I Think, Therefore I Learn!

Graham Foster

Evelyn Sawicki

Hyacinth Schaeffer

Victor Zelinski

Pembroke Publishers Limited

The authors wish to thank the following people for specific advice and contributions to the project:
Liz Donovan,
Dr. Karen Kovach,
Michael Schaeffer,
and Janeen Werner-King.

© 2002 Pembroke Publishers
538 Hood Road
Markham, Ontario, Canada L3R 3K9
www.pembrokepublishers.com

Distributed in the U.S. by Stenhouse Publishers
477 Congress Street
Portland, ME 04101
www.stenhouse.com

We acknowledge the financial support of the Government of Canada through the Book Publishing Industry Development Program (BPIDP) for our publishing activities.

National Library of Canada Cataloguing in Publication

Main entry under title:
    I think, therefore I learn! / Graham Foster ... [et. al.].

Includes bibliographical references and index.
ISBN 1-55138-148-6

1. Study skills.   I. Foster, Graham

LB3013.P38 2002   371.3   C2002-902792-6

Editor: Kate Revington
Cover Design: John Zehethofer
Typesetting: Jay Tee Graphics

Printed and bound in Canada
9 8 7 6 5 4 3 2 1

Contents

1 A Powerful Way of Thinking

Students naturally approach learning tasks in many different ways. Some students aim to get through their learning tasks as quickly and painlessly as possible. They do their work with little regard for options and alternatives—they often seem to be operating by rote. Some students prefer constant direction and guidance to complete tasks. They want to know that they are on the right track, and they expect the teacher to tell them exactly what to do next. Still other students are willing to explore different possibilities or options for getting work done. They may consider how their learning strengths, preferences, and background knowledge will help them succeed in the task. This latter group of students is the most *metacognitive*.

In the past few years, many curriculum developers and textbook writers have placed an increasing emphasis on metacognition. Although teachers are always aware of such helpful curriculum trends, those who have been giving their teaching a metacognitive dimension would likely do so whether prescribed curriculum documents and resources recognized it or not. These teachers know that students are more successful when they are metacognitive.

So, just what does that mean? Before considering key aspects in detail, let's unpack the word "metacognition." *Cognition* refers to the process of knowing. *Meta,* derived from the Greek, means beyond or from. Metacognition, then, refers to knowing how we learn best and consciously controlling our learning—which is surely what we want for our students.

Analyzing Tasks

What do metacognitive students do? Possibly the most important thing is that they analyze what they have to do and do that often. *What do I have to do? What are my options and strategies? How well did my choices work? What might I keep or change for next time?* Opportunities for task analysis include informal conferences between the student and teachers as well as between the student and peers. Students may also analyze tasks through written comments made throughout a task or project. You can encourage such thinking by inviting students to reflect before, during, and after their assessments. Students thus learn to think about their thinking.

How can teachers foster task analysis? Here are some of the many ways.

• Show students examples of work related to the task—print, recorded, or videotaped.
• Have students confirm their understanding of a task by explaining it to peers or putting it into their own words on paper.
• Encourage students to identify their strengths and, for group tasks, the strengths of other members as these relate to task completion.
• Encourage students to brainstorm options and seek advice or information from print and non-print resources, as well as from other people, about options and strategies for completing a task.
• Involve students in the creation of rubrics.
• Provide time for students to note personal learning goals—possibly on a chart titled "Goals Achieved/Goals Still to Be Achieved."

Self-Regulating Learning

A key characteristic of metacognition is self-regulation of one's learning. Metacognitive learners think about their choices, monitor the effectiveness of their choices, and regularly set goals for future learning. Non-metacognitive learners depend excessively on directions from others, complete tasks with little or no regard to alternatives, and seldom set goals for future learning.

The following chart sets out extreme differences between metacognitive and non-metacognitive learners. Most students will fall between the extremes presented.

Metacognitive Learners	Non-metacognitive Learners
• Describe their strengths as learners	• Are unaware of their strengths as learners
• Analyze learning tasks to consider options	• Complete learning tasks by rote
• Explain their choices in completing learning tasks	• Complete learning tasks without explaining their approach to the task

Metacognitive Learners	Non-metacognitive Learners
• Monitor the effectiveness of choices during and following the learning activity	• Pay little attention to their choices in learning
• Regularly set goals for learning	• Do not set goals for future learning

Knowing Yourself

Knowing yourself as a learner, that is, knowing your strengths and preferences in learning, is a critical characteristic of the metacognitive learner.

Teachers, as well as students, can explore the importance of understanding themselves as learners by thinking about these questions:

1. *What do I find easy to learn?*
2. *What do I find difficult to learn?*
3. *What conditions help me to learn challenging materials?*

Reflect on these questions. How would you answer them? Do you think others might differ in their answers? Of course they will! If you doubt this, discuss the questions in a small group. Doing so has particular value for groups of teachers who are learning about metacognition.

At workshops, teachers often mention that they find something easy to learn when they have background for the learning and when they are confident with the subject matter. They indicate that when they have little background or confidence, the learning is difficult. For example, some teachers will say that learning something new about history is easier than learning something new about mathematics due to their background and confidence.

Responses to the third question are especially interesting. They reveal that learners employ different strategies, especially when they confront challenging material. Teachers might mention a favorite approach, such as creating a chart or diagram or using hands-on materials. They often emphasize the importance of having access to someone they trust to help them with difficult learning. What works for one person does not work for another, but successful learners know what works best for them.

The third question enters the territory of metacognition, where you discover how you learn best and how you deal with challenges. This question also leads teachers to reflect on how they can assist students to discover and use those learning strategies and options that work best for them.

Teachers who are familiar with Howard Gardner's work on multiple intelligences will note an obvious link between multiple intelligences and metacognition. It is useful for teachers and students to recognize and encourage a variety of intelligences that can be employed to complete tasks. If students recognize intellectual strength in linguistic, logical-mathematical, spatial, bodily-kinesthetic, musical, interpersonal, intrapersonal, naturalistic, or environmental forms, their self-knowledge will help them complete tasks and to divide the labour wisely during group work. The question *How will my strengths as a learner help me and possibly my group complete this task?* is valued by advocates of multiple intelligences and metacognition alike.

How Important Is Metacognition?

Metacognition has a critical role to play in many areas, including school, employment, and personal life. Before affirming the value of what is essentially thinking about thinking, though, one issue must be dealt with. Many students may do well in school without being particularly metacognitive. Does that reality diminish the value of metacognition? No.

An essential tool for challenging tasks

One of the authors of this book worked with a group of teachers who wondered about this latter question. The teachers decided to coordinate instruction to foster metacognition in reading in their elementary school. Early in the year, they administered a reading comprehension test, as well as a survey that required students to identify favorite reading strategies. Several students who scored highly on the reading comprehension test were unable to identify strategies that worked well for them. Teachers wondered whether these successful students would benefit from an emphasis on metacognition since they were already doing well. Why bother adding a metacognitive dimension?

At the end of the year, the teachers concluded that metacognitive reading benefited *all* students in the class. A parallel test was given. The same students who did best earlier proved to be far more capable of identifying preferred reading strategies.

Struggling learners benefit from an emphasis on metacognition, but so do gifted learners. In a *Gifted Child Quarterly* article titled "What Gifted Students Can Learn," Thomas Scruggs and colleagues reported that increases in learning have followed direct instruction in metacognitive strategies and that independence develops gradually. Metacognition rewards learners when the task challenges them and when an automatic or intuitive response is not enough. The successful young readers described above will confront texts in the future that will require them to know and select from a repertoire of strategies. With certain texts, *all* of us are remedial readers.

A means to meet desired learning outcomes

Metacognition helps students meet what many educators view as tough curriculum expectations. For example, students are increasingly required to compose, to solve problems, to complete experiments, to defend positions on a variety of issues, and more. Since curriculum guidelines are usually non-negotiable, teachers need to provide students with strong ways to meet them. As students learn to think about their thinking, they learn more actively, decisively, and reflectively.

In a sense, metacognition involves challenging students to take responsibility for their learning: they do this by discovering strategies that work best for them. Teachers encourage metacognition when they recognize the viability of several approaches to complete a task. Those who always insist on a single approach—probably that which works best for them—discourage metacognition. In reflecting on metacognition, teachers have often pointed out that they will continue to teach and to model strategies that students can use to complete tasks, for example, the use of graphic organizers to plan writing. However, they will invite students to suggest and use alternatives and modifications. More than that, they will encourage students to employ the strategy that works best for them.

A benefit to classroom atmosphere

A group of senior high teachers agreed to promote metacognition across grades and subjects in their urban school. They reported a surprising benefit to their shared commitment. Although initially students resisted efforts to have them take more ownership of their learning, as time went by and teachers persisted, students became increasingly reflective. Teachers noted that as students became less dependent on them for direction, classroom management became easier, disciplinary issues declined, and time on-task improved. Classroom atmosphere improved, as well as quality of student work.

A way to develop skills valued for work

The Conference Board of Canada, an association of leading Canadian educational and business organizations, suggests that metacognitive students demonstrate life skills that will serve them well in their employment years. In a document titled Employability Skills 2000+, it notes the following skills under this heading: "The skills you will need to enter, stay in, and progress in the world of work—whether you work on your own or as part of a team." Below are selected fundamental and personal management skills that resonate with metacognition.

Think & Solve Problems
- Assess situations and identify problems.
- Seek different points of view and evaluate them based on facts.
- Be creative and innovative in exploring possible solutions.
- Evaluate solutions to make recommendations or decisions.
- Check to see if a solution works, and act on opportunities for improvement.

Learn continuously
- Set your own learning goals.
- Identify and access learning sources and opportunities.
- Plan for and achieve your learning goals.

The Conference Board statement implicitly warns students that quickly selecting an option to complete a task or depending regularly on a supervisor to direct work will not serve them well. To have successful careers, they will have to systematically explore options to complete tasks, reflect on how well their choices work, and set goals related to learning from their experiences. The characteristics noted are important descriptors of metacognition.

A way to cultivate citizenship

Just as metacognition benefits employment prospects, it promotes responsible citizenship. Effective involvement in social issues depends on a thorough issue analysis, where various points of view are assessed; an exploration of options or choices; and a weighing of costs and benefits to various choices before decisions are made. Citizenship depends upon a willingness to become informed and a willingness to become involved: these are both hallmarks of metacognition. Chapter 5 elaborates on this theme.

A way to understand yourself

Even more important than its value to employment and citizenship, metacognition relates to what many people would see as the most important mission in their lives—self-understanding. When people in the midst of tasks think about their preferences, strengths, and goals, they come to know themselves as persons, to understand their similarities and differences to others. It is possible to complete tasks without reflection. However, if you value self-understanding, as you face the tasks of life and, indeed, when you determine which tasks are most worth pursuing, you will take time to think about your preferences, strengths, and goals.

A means to hone instructional practice

Beyond having value for your students, taking a metacognitive approach allows you, as a teacher, to improve your teaching practices. The characteristics of metacognitive learners apply equally to metacognitive teachers: the abilities to describe strengths, to analyze instructional tasks, to articulate choices for a group of students, to monitor consistently the effectiveness of their choices, and to set goals for future instruction for the class. It can be argued that effective teaching is a metacognitive act.

Fostering a Metacognitive Approach

Teachers who attempt to control all of their students' learning processes could well be teaching strategies without helping students become metacognitive. Imagine a classroom in which a teacher directs the reading of a text. First, the class is directed to a reading purpose. Then the class is directed to predict the text's theme from an illustration. After students read to a certain point, the teacher directs them to summarize what they have read. Setting a purpose for reading, predicting, and summarizing are powerful reading strategies; however, until these strategies have been selected and controlled by students rather than teachers, students are not being metacognitive. They need to control their own learning.

Modelling strategies and flexible thinking

Do not expect students to learn strategies by osmosis, though. Guided reading of texts and modelling of strategies by teachers are critically important for students to learn about strategies and options. An emphasis on metacognition places a special accent on direct instruction: attention to options and possibilities. For example, you could ask: "What different reading purposes might be appropriate for this text? Besides predicting and summarizing, what strategies might you use to read with purpose?"

Even with a focus on a selected strategy, you should help students recognize that readers predict and visualize differently. For example, to help them see this, you could use the "unfolding method" with a short text, possibly a poem. Ask students to cover the text with a piece of blank paper. Following your directions, have students uncover, or unfold, the text bit by bit. You might choose to have them read to the end of the first sentence in a poem (if the poem has punctuation). Then ask students to predict what comes next or to summarize or sketch what they see in the unfolded section. It quickly becomes apparent that while predictions and visualizations vary from student to student, predicting and visualizing are valuable reading strategies.

In the modelling of strategies, you can encourage metacognition when you think aloud about "what works for me." For instance, a teacher shared with a class the observation that a thought map or thought web worked better for him than an outline when he was planning expository writing. He told the story that when he was forced to submit outlines in school, he often wrote the essay first and then completed the outline. He then demonstrated one or two favorite thought webs. In the spirit of metacognition, he inquired whether some students preferred outlines. A few students expressed their preference for outlines rather than webs.

The implicit message is that modelled strategies might also work well for certain students with certain tasks, but that students must *discover* what works for them. Instead of constantly saying, "Do this," say, "This is what I'm doing now for this particular task. What else could I do to complete the task?" In discussing and modelling alternative strategies, and in showing students how you deal with challenges and uncertainties, you foster metacognition.

Metacognitive instruction acknowledges the vulnerability of the learner as well as the power of well-chosen strategies in dealing with that vulnerability. You can demonstrate to students the value of recognizing the intelligences that are your strengths and how you can use your strength in certain intelligences to help you complete tasks and to work with others to complete tasks.

As mentioned earlier, students are often resistant to metacognition at first: some students would rather not take responsibility for their learning. The key to overcoming resistance is to demonstrate that students can do better work when they are metacognitive. Since students often heed peers more than teachers, it may be helpful in a given task for students to share what they have done and how they have done it.

Encouraging thoughtful work

In all subjects and in all grades, teachers' instructional strategies will encourage students' thinking about the best ways to complete learning tasks. The following list, a summary of points elaborated in this chapter, notes specific instructional strategies designed so that students may improve how they regulate their own learning.

- Model strategies with an emphasis on *"What works for me . . . "* and *"What else could I do?"* Encourage students to model strategies for other students.
- Encourage students to analyze tasks and to select strategies and skills to complete tasks. (See "Thinking About My Work Written Response" on pages 14 and 15 for

a valuable student form that can be used to guide analysis of specific tasks in many grades and subjects.)

- Invite students to reflect on how well their choices and strategies have worked throughout their efforts to complete the task.
- Encourage students to learn about their strengths and learning preferences and to comment about themselves as learners.
- Include student self-assessment (see "Student and Teacher Assessment Checklist" on pages 16 and 17 bearing in mind that this versatile form for prompting reflection is intended mainly to monitor growth and development); call for goal setting.

The key word "encourage" underlines that teachers cannot force students to think about their thinking; they can only nurture it and guide it in their students. They should also appreciate that students are far more likely to become metacognitive if thinking about thinking is encouraged at home as well as at school. Schools are wise to use information sessions, parent-teacher conferences, and newsletters to foster parental support. Also, a form such as "A Parental Guide to Promoting Reflective Learning" (see pages 87–88) may help. Students vary in their willingness and ability to be metacognitive; however, you will gain great professional satisfaction when more students are more metacognitive more often.

Weighing pluses and minuses with colleagues

A worthwhile professional development activity for teachers is to work together to list advantages and disadvantages of metacognition in their school's instructional program.

Typically, teachers mention benefits for students, such as divergent thinking, deeper understanding of strategies, greater confidence and independence, and improved classroom climate.

Overwhelmingly, the negative list usually focuses on time. Metacognition develops slowly and therefore promoting it demands time within a crowded curriculum. While items are constantly added to mandated programs, they are seldom deleted. Teachers are wise to address the fundamental management question about metacognition: Is it worth the time? They need to be convinced that, while progress may be slow at first, over time, student learning will be much improved when students take increased responsibility for their learning.

A group of high school English Language Arts teachers decided to co-coordinate implementation of metacognition across the grades. They decided that each teacher would revise a favorite unit of work to emphasize metacognition. These revised units were subsequently discussed at a workshop with a focus on the question: How much time will an emphasis on metacognition demand with this unit? The teachers realized that their understanding of metacognition prompts them to

Thinking About My Work
Written Response

Criteria Appropriate for This Task ✓	Thinking About My Work
	1. I have a good idea of what I am supposed to do and I can explain it in my own words. In this task I am asked to _____ _____ _____
	2. I can think of and list different ways to complete this task. Another way I could complete this task: _____ _____ _____
	3. I can describe my plan for completing the task. Here is my plan: _____ _____ _____
	4. I have selected or adapted methods, approaches, or strategies I have used before to help me complete this task. Something I did before that helped me decide how to complete this task: _____ _____ _____

5. I have considered my strengths and learning preferences to complete this task.

One strength or learning preference that I will use to complete this assignment is

_____

_____

_____

_____

6. I have considered different ways in which to communicate my work.

One way to show/tell other people what I did is to

_____

_____

Another way would be to

_____

_____

_____

_____

7. I have focused on my personal learning goal of

_____

_____

_____

Next time I need to complete a task like this I will

_____

_____

_____

8. _____

_____

_____

_____

_____

_____

Student and Teacher Assessment Checklist

Name of Task _____ Student Name _____

Criteria Appropriate for This Task ✓	Thinking About My Work	Student Assessment ✓	Teacher Assessment ✓
	1. I have a good idea of what I am supposed to do and I can explain it in my own words.		
	2. I can think of and list different ways to do this task.		
	3. I have considered how my strengths and learning preferences will help me complete this task.		
	4. I can describe my plan for completing the task.		
	5. I understand how my work will be marked.		
	6. I am able to use the scoring guide (rubric) to evaluate my own work and the work of others.		
	7. I have used a method that I have seen my teacher use.		
	8. I have adapted methods I have used before to help me complete this task.		

Criteria Appropriate for This Task ✓	Thinking About My Work	Student Assessment ✓	Teacher Assessment ✓
	9. In completing my task, I have considered the following questions: • What did I do? • What could I have done instead? • What will I do next time?		
	10. My plan worked and I can explain why.		
	11. I have considered different ways in which to communicate my work.		
	12. I have considered my personal learning goals to improve my work on this task.		
	13.		
	14.		
	15.		

encourage it every day with a variety of tasks. They agreed that the extra time required at first would probably be time well spent.

Below is a brief summary of the pluses and minuses associated with metacognition.

Pluses	Minuses
• Students' commitment to learning	• Time required
• Improved work over time	• Resistance from students and some colleagues
• More thinking about strategies	• Resistance from parents who stress a "right answer" approach to schooling
• Improved self-confidence	• Lack of emphasis in many learning resources used in schools
• Increased independence	
• Improved classroom atmosphere	

Making Students Aware of Strategies

Being metacognitive in learning skills specified in mandated curricula means being aware of the strategies or options available in completing tasks. Students benefit when they learn that strategies refer to the "know how" of successful practitioners—effective readers, writers, social scientists, scientists, mathematicians, hairdressers, athletes, and so on. As a teacher, you are wise to help students understand the importance and meaning of the word "strategies." While skills refer to *what* students are expected to learn, strategies refer to *how* students complete learning tasks.

Teachers need to be clear about skills and strategies across grades and subjects. They can thereby help students explore two significant metacognitive questions in their completion of learning tasks:

1. *How can I go about completing this task?* (strategies)
2. *What abilities do I need to activate or develop to complete this task?* (skills)

Many teachers have studied Bloom's taxonomy to reflect on skills required in specific learning and to plan for higher order thinking skills. Bloom's taxonomy presents a hierarchy of thinking skills, including knowledge, comprehension, application, analysis, synthesis, and evaluation. Learning about the level of thinking required in a specific learning task—especially through examples of effective student work—should help students understand the requirements of the task as well as to consider options and strategies that may be helpful in completing the task.

Several sources on metacognition stress that considering both strategies and skills benefits learners throughout the learning process—not simply at the planning stage. Students should select and monitor options when they analyze a learning task, when they plan their work, when they work their plan, and when they reflect on the final product. *What strategies and skills did I employ? How well did they work? What might I keep or change for next time?*

Providing Students with Choice

In response to the reality of ever-widening ranges of student ability in the classroom, many educational organizations have emphasized differentiated instruction over the past several years. A major theme of differentiated instruction is planning for the varied learning needs of students in the class. Consider how metacognition might enhance each of the following possibilities for differentiation: differentiated assignments, resources, learning activities, time allotments to complete tasks, assessment, and degrees of mediation or assistance to individual students (provided by the teacher, other adults, and peers). Students' involvement in decisions about differentiation makes the choices metacognitive. When students enjoy a measure of decision making about their assignments, about the print, human, and media resources they will use to complete them, and about the options and strategies they will choose to fulfil those assignments, they are empowered to take responsibility for their own learning.

Differentiated instruction implies that students will complete self-assessment and goal-setting tasks related to their own learning goals. Individual students will vary in self-assessment criteria and will set individual goals. Differentiated self-assessment and goal setting are *metacognitive* self-assessment and goal setting.

Helping students understand their strengths as learners and employ these strengths to complete learning tasks fosters metacognition. For instance, if the learning expectations focus on techniques used to persuade, visual learners might prefer to analyze videos or print advertisements; auditory learners might work with songs or tape-recorded speeches; kinesthetic learners might dramatize persuasive techniques. If they were organizing a persuasive essay, verbal learners might prefer to use a traditional outline; visual learners, on the other hand, would probably select a graphic organizer. The message to teachers is clear: In completing educational requirements, students benefit when they understand themselves as learners *and* when they are able to employ their strengths.

Assessing Performance Using Relevant Criteria

The increasing emphasis on performance assessment, evident in several disciplines, also argues for metacognition.

A general review of forms of assessment may be useful here. Essentially, a teacher has three options for assessment as illustrated by the following chart:

Assessment Type	Definition	Examples
Observation	Informal, sometimes casual assessment of students often rotationally scheduled and focused	• Anecdotal records • Observations of students working in groups • Checklists
Pre-specified Response	Assessment that requires students to approximate a predetermined response	• Multiple choice • Short answer • True/False • Matching • Dictation • Numeric responses
Performance Assessment	Formal assessment that demands the use of criteria which are communicated directly to learners and used as guidelines by both students and teachers	• Analytical or holistic forms for marking and representing • Rubrics for projects, research, experimental design, role play, debate, and writing

As a challenge, examine any recently developed curriculum or program document that you are expected to implement. How many expectations or outcomes imply observation for assessment? How many imply pre-specified response? How many imply performance? All forms of assessment are required. However, you will probably notice that performance assessment is required for many, if not most, of the expectations or outcomes.

Metacognition matters more than ever because it makes students' performances better. For example, dramatic performance improves when actors and directors consider appropriate gestures, movements, and voice features. What are the options? Which options work most effectively? These questions are metacognitive. On the other hand, a metacognitive approach alone is not enough. A student who is preparing an oral interpretation of literature, for example, would also need to have a sense of the emotional meaning of the piece. This understanding would affect choices about tone, volume, speed of delivery, words emphasized, gesture, and eye contact.

Performance assessment demands the use of criteria related to the assignment's purpose. Examples of learning activities that require performance assessment include acting, the composition and performance of music, artistic compositions, problem solving, research, readers' theatre, debating, oral interpretation of literature, audio-visual presentations, and all forms of written composition. Students perform better when they know the criteria for effective performance.

An emphasis on metacognition challenges students to use exemplars, or examples of effective performances, to identify appropriate criteria. In many classrooms, students work with teachers to develop rubrics and self-assessment forms for performances. These rubrics and self-assessment forms become even more metacognitive when they call upon students to include personal learning goals as criteria. Students perform better when they practise and refine their work before they present it. Practice and refinement are characterized by reflection on options, choices, and consequences—by metacognition.

The following chart, from *Student Self-Assessment,* illustrates how student self-assessment can be given a metacognitive dimension. Here, a student may list criteria related to personal learning goals for working in small groups. A blank form appears on page 86 as an appendix.

Small-Group Work Student Assessment Form

	Criteria	*My Goals for Small-Group Work*
✓	1. I helped the group review its task.	*My goal is to continue to work as well as I worked with my group on this project.*
___	2. I contributed relevant ideas; I stayed on topic.	
✓	3. I listened carefully to other group members.	
✓	4. I was open-minded about differ-ent interpretations or understandings.	
✓	5. I helped the group stay focused on its task.	
✓	6. I contributed to the summary which concluded the group work.	
✓	7. I encouraged all members of the group to contribute.	

Teachers may choose to employ a related instructional approach to encourage metacognitive self-assessment by students. Have students regularly update a "Goals

Achieved/Goals Still to Be Achieved" page in their work folders or portfolios for different subjects. The primary grades version of this page could be labelled

Can Do	Need to Do

The following example suggests that completing such a goals chart encourages students to be reflective and to take ownership of their learning.

My Personal Learning Goals	
Name _Mary Brownley_	
Subject _Language Arts_	Grade _9_
Goals Achieved	**Goals Still to Be Achieved**
• *Writing is organized appropriately.* • *Words are colourful.* • *fewer spelling mistakes* • *correct use of apostrophe*	• *to write convincing dialogue* • *to have "smooth" use of quotations in writing* • *to improve use of commas*

Taking a Fresh Look at Familiar Instructional Models

An emphasis on metacognition may challenge you, as an educator, to take a fresh look at the process, inquiry, and problem-solving models in vogue for several years. As useful as such models have been in suggesting learning sequences, educators have sometimes reduced them to recipe-like formulae.

Below is a summary of these instructional models.

Reading Process Model: A model that breaks the act of reading into pre-reading, during-reading, and post-reading stages with an emphasis on strategies employed by successful readers at each of these stages

Writing Process Model: A model that breaks the act of writing into pre-writing, drafting, revision, and publication stages with an emphasis on strategies employed by successful writers at each of these stages

Problem-Solving Model: A model that breaks problem solving into five steps: (1) understanding the problem, (2) devising the plan, (3) carrying out a plan, (4) looking back at one's solution and process, and (5) communicating the solution

Inquiry Model: A model of instruction that engages students in the search for solutions for problems in society

Scientific Inquiry Model: A model that involves making observations; posing questions; examining sources of information; planning investigations; gathering, analyzing, and interpreting data; proposing answers, explanations, and predictions; and communicating results

A metacognitive viewpoint has little patience for the notion that there is one writing process, one problem-solving model, and one inquiry model that works with cookie-cutter efficiency for all learners all the time. An emphasis on metacognition reminds educators that learners should adapt processes and models to particular tasks and should apply strategies that work best for them in their learning.

Teachers who know the content of subject disciplines and the skills and strategies important in these disciplines can promote subject-specific metacognitive practices better than teachers working outside their area of expertise. Indeed, as noted in *How People Learn*, "The teaching of metacognitive activities must be incorporated into the subject matter that people are learning (White and Frederickson, 1998). These strategies are not generic across subjects, and attempts to teach them as generic lead to failure to transfer" (2000, 19).

Subsequent chapters consider specific applications and examples related to language arts, mathematics, science, and social studies. They will illustrate that solid, familiar practice in these subject disciplines can be enriched when teachers consciously emphasize metacognition in their instruction.

Learning to Think, Thinking to Learn: Factsheet

All of us have tasks to complete, but some of us complete them better. Why? One answer might be that we have learned to think about our thinking before, during, and after working on the task. We have learned to think responsibly, or, as some might say, we have learned to think *metacognitively*.

What does this mean more precisely? The term *metacognition* means thoughtful analysis and monitoring of a task. When students actively think about how best to do something, they consider as many options as they can as well as their own relevant strengths and interests. Teachers who nurture this approach will recognize that for many learning tasks, students do not need to work in the same way. They will also realize that skills and strategies are learned and transferred most effectively when connected to a specific task.

Once students begin to focus on how they are achieving something, they gain insights into themselves as learners. They also become more responsible for their learning, taking ownership of it. Therefore, it is important and desirable that students learn to take a metacognitive approach to learning.

Teachers foster metacognition in their students when they ask and encourage them

- to explain the learning task in their own words
- to express what they plan to do before, during, and after the work
- to consider which of their personal strengths and interests are relevant to completing the task
- to set goals for future learning based on assessing what worked best this time and what they think they should keep or change
- to explain what working through the task taught them about themselves as learners

Teachers can also model the metacognitive approach for their students:

- expressing aloud in words their thoughts about how to complete a task
- identifying options and strategies available to complete the task
- choosing among and acting upon the options and strategies

Thinking responsibly about how to complete a task is a critically important life skill for all of us. It is required for more successful academic studies, in demand in the workplace, needed for "good" citizenship, and valued in the development of the whole person. Metacognition, although an unfamiliar term perhaps, is the powerful way of thinking that enables us to better achieve our learning and living potential.

2 Language Arts: A Way to Know Self and World

As language arts programs have been revised and implemented over the past few decades, these programs have strongly emphasized the connection between language and learning. In the 1970s and 1980s language arts programs recognized that language is much more than a matter of effective communication; it is also critical for representing reality, thinking, and constructing personal knowledge. These curricula stressed that frequent language use for varied purposes and audiences and for exploring content is important for students in all subject disciplines, not only language arts. The word "metacognition" was not emphasized in language arts curriculum documents of the 1970s and 1980s. However, it appears prominently in several recent language arts curriculum documents and prescribed sources.

Moving Beyond Language to Learn

Why is the word "metacognition" surfacing now? In a sense, the recent emphasis on metacognition complements and extends previous attention to language and learning themes. After all, metacognitive learners regulate and think about their learning. They learn from the consequences of their choices. They benefit from talking through their options and strategies in completing tasks. Using language to learn is the foundation of using it to communicate effectively.

The current emphasis on metacognition relates squarely to practical realities as well as to learning theory. Business leaders, as well as educators, stress that task analysis, independent thinking, and problem solving are the bases for success in careers, so they should be emphasized more strongly in language arts curricula. Therefore, recently developed language arts programs have complemented earlier language-to-learn themes with attention to metacognition.

From a language arts perspective, metacognition makes sense on an idealistic, as well as a practical, career-oriented plane. For decades, language arts programs have emphasized the personal benefits of reading and writing as well as those of the other language arts. Reading and writing are, of course, lenses on the self, powerful methods to understand self and world, to decide what is important in life and what is unimportant. Many authors have observed that writing is a matter of discovering meaning and unpacking experiences as much as it is about communicating with readers.

In an article titled "The Acid Test for Literature Instruction," Louise Rosenblatt raised these still timely questions about the personal relevance of reading.

> Does this practice or approach hinder or foster a sense that literature exists as a form of personally meaningful experiences? Is the pupil's interaction with the literary work itself the center from which all else radiates? Is the student being helped to grow in a relationship of integrity to language and literature? Is he building a lifetime habit of significant reading? (1956, 74)

Anyone who believes that one's most important mission in life is self-understanding and that language and literature foster self-understanding will applaud current attention to metacognition. After all, a critical component of understanding oneself is understanding how one learns effectively, and effective learning differs from person to person.

Refining Strategies and Models

An emphasis on metacognition refines another recent curriculum emphasis in language arts: strategies and process models. Chapter 1 emphasized the importance of strategies in metacognitive learning. (Note that this chapter uses the words "process" and "strategy" synonymously. Both words refer to a learner's know-how about completing tasks, whether or not this know-how is effective.) Here we look at providing strategies and process models with a metacognitive dimension.

Strategies for reading

Language arts professional literature frequently describes a viable reading process according to what effective readers often do before, during, and after reading. Strategies noted below are often mentioned.

BEFORE READING

These strategies recognize that successful readers must fit what is in the text to what they already know about the subject of the text.

- Activating/building background knowledge: Someone familiar with curling, for example, will have the background to make sense of references to "hog lines," "hacks," "skip," "house," and "button"; someone unfamiliar with curling would benefit from building background to foster comprehension.
- Setting purpose: Purpose might be to gather information, to locate a specific fact, or to infer character traits. It provides a focus for reading.
- Predicting or questioning: This activity also provides a focus for reading.

DURING READING

These strategies vary according to the text being read as well as the reader's preferences.

- Visualizing, or envisioning: This strategy refers to the benefit of picturing or "running the movie in one's mind" as one reads.
- Chunking text: This refers to looking for units of thought, such as sentences, stanzas, or paragraphs.
- Predicting and questioning: Effective readers often wonder what will follow in a text and express their wondering in a prediction or question. "I think that the butler did it." (Prediction) "Is someone other than the butler guilty?" (Question)
- Linking text to personal experience: This linking to personal experience is related to activating background knowledge. Personal experience of betrayal should help one understand and judge how well betrayal is presented in a novel.
- Monitoring for meaning: Effective readers will deal with something that does not make sense to them by checking back in the text or checking a dictionary or other reference.
- Summarizing or paraphrasing: Putting a text in their own words allows effective readers to work out the essential meaning of the text.

AFTER READING

These strategies overlap with strategies at other stages in the process.

- Summarizing
- Checking predictions
- Answering questions
- Checking to refine interpretations: Successful readers do not settle on meaning too quickly; they interpret meaning and check the text to refine their interpretation. On multiple-choice readings tests, this strategy would take the form of checking the text before settling on one of the options for a question.

A metacognitive perspective emphasizes that readers who consciously employ these strategies and vary their use of them depending on the text do better in their reading. This is especially so when they confront a text that is personally challenging. Readers benefit when they discover the strategies that work best for them and when they thoughtfully select strategies for specific texts. Bess Hinson noted this in *New Directions in Reading Instruction,* published by the International Reading Association.

> The more students are aware of the processes and strategies that they are employing, the more successful they will be at applying these processes and skills. Students' ability to monitor their own reading process, metacognition, is a key factor in achieving reading success. As students practice self-monitoring, they become aware of their own ways of processing knowledge (2000, 10).

Strategies for writing

A writing process approach can also be considered according to what effective writers do often before, during, and after drafting text.

BEFORE DRAFTING

These strategies recognize that writers need to discover and to focus what they have to say in a composition.

- Activating/building background knowledge about topic and form for the composition
- Engaging in exploratory writing: sometimes called free-writing or journal writing, this kind of writing focuses on discovery rather than communication. (Sometimes, ideas or experiences revealed through exploratory writing can be taken to final draft.)
- Determining writing variables: variables include purpose, audience, format, topic, and role for the writing.
- Choosing a pre-writing approach: alternatives include using graphic organizers, brainstorming, completing research notes, and free-writing.

DURING DRAFTING

These strategies remind writers to "keep the flow going."

- Writing on every other line: doing this encourages revision.
- Beginning at the most comfortable part of the composition: writers are reminded that writing sequence is a personal choice and that writers often write the introduction last.
- Leaving blank spaces when words don't come: it's more important to get ideas on paper than to refine expression.
- Rereading what one has written before continuing the draft
- Referring to pre-writing notes and modifying them

AFTER DRAFTING

Strategies remind students that effective writers learn to be their own readers.

- Rereading for clarity: writers should focus on the clarity of their expression and organization, on their vocabulary and sentence pattern choices, and on matters of spelling, punctuation, and grammar usage.
- Conferring with others to improve the writing: some writers prefer to revise with partner help; others do not.
- Applying specific criteria appropriate to purpose, audience, format, topic, and role for the writing

As with reading process, a metacognitive perspective on writing process emphasizes that the know-how of effective writers is personal, not universal. Writers discover what works best for them as individuals and adapt strategies to the requirements of a specific composition. However, as George Hillocks writes in *Research on Written Composition, New Directions in Teaching,* "We do know from a variety of sources that writing is recursive, with writers moving back to what has been written and forward to what has not" (1986, 60).

If students are always required to use strategies as a formula, they are not being metacognitive. Of course, teachers want students to try a variety of strategies, and students cannot choose and use strategies that they don't know. Still, as they do learning tasks throughout the year, students become better at analyzing tasks and in independently choosing and monitoring strategies to complete these tasks. From the earliest grades in school, students should be able to describe strategies employed to complete tasks, to expand their repertoire of strategies, and to regularly set goals about their use of strategies. If teachers constantly directly students in their use of strategies, the learning may be described as strategic, but not metacognitive. The metacognitive metaphor for the teacher is *guide* rather than director.

How to Promote Metacognition in Language Arts

Language arts teachers have a powerful motivation to promote metacognition—students' reading, writing, and oral language skills benefit. They can support and guide students' metacognition, but cannot direct it. Given that, how can they help students to be metacognitive? Here are four keys:

- Model strategies.
- Encourage task analysis.
- Add a metacognitive dimension to familiar language arts practice.
- Emphasize metacognition in language arts assessment.

Model Strategies

The modelling of strategies by language arts teachers and by students should emphasize possibilities rather than narrow choice or the idea that the model is the only way to complete the task.

The following story illustrates the point. In the orientation of a revised language arts program in a major school district, in-service leaders tried to demonstrate how modelling should be given a metacognitive dimension. The orientation session focused on two topics: the outcomes influence on curriculum, considered in the first hour; and metacognition, considered in the second. To explore the outcomes approach, in-service leaders deliberately used the familiar K-W-L strategy in a non-metacognitive way. In this strategy, students list what they know about a topic (K), what they think they will learn about a topic (W) and, following study, what they have learned about the topic (L). In-service leaders directed 1,500 teachers in on-site sessions in 87 schools to explore the outcomes philosophy using K-W-L. They directed teachers to write what they knew about outcomes, what they thought they would learn about outcomes and, following the presentations, to record what they had actually learned about the outcomes approach. When the teachers considered metacognition in the second half of the session, in-service leaders questioned whether the use of K-W-L earlier was metacognitive. Clearly, it was not since the strategy was employed so directly.

In helping colleagues learn about outcomes philosophy, the learning task for the first half of the session, in-service leaders should certainly have modelled K-W-L and suggested it as a possibility to complete the learning task. To make a point, in-service leaders did not encourage metacognition—they presented K-W-L as the *only* strategy. They would have fostered metacognition much more had they said: "Our task is to learn about outcomes. K-W-L is one way. What other ways could we use to explore outcomes? What would work most effectively for *you*?"

The metacognitive way of modelling strategies shows an openness to alternatives and challenges learners to think about what works best for them personally. Metacognitive modelling says: "Here's one way to do it. How else could we do it? Use the strategy that works best for you."

When it comes to strategy, students need choice. Consider the way that students were once required to complete outlines. Can you recall being required to complete and submit an outline for an essay? You were probably told that the outline helped you to organize your writing. Scores of teachers have admitted that, when outlines were required, they wrote the essay first and completed the outlines afterwards! Obviously, the outline fell short as a personal pre-writing strategy. With a metacognitive approach, students would be challenged to consider the pre-writing approach that would work best for them. For certain students in certain assignments, a thought web might work better. Others might profit more by completing a Venn diagram, others by free-writing about the topic. Indeed, some students for certain assignments might choose the outline as a productive pre-writing strategy. For them, the use of the outline would be metacognitive. The reason is that they chose the outline rather than being required to complete it.

Encourage Task Analysis

Language arts teachers should also encourage students to analyze their tasks. There are many ways of doing so. Check page 6 for a summary of general methods. To promote metacognition, invite students to articulate which method might work effectively for them personally for the task at hand.

For composition assignments, in particular, you might suggest that students review an acronym, such as RAFTS. As noted in Chapter 1, in an upper elementary school that focused on metacognition in writing, teachers asked students in October and in May to write down what worked best for them in focusing and planning their writing. Across the grades, students could list few approaches in October; by May, their lists were more extensive, with much variation. Most students mentioned use of RAFTS.

Role	From whose point of view am I writing—my own or someone else's?
Audience	To whom am I writing? To a specific individual or group or a general audience? What is my relationship to this audience?
Format	What form is appropriate for my writing—editorial, narrative, poem, description?
Topic	What am I writing about?
Strong Verb	What strong verb specifically expresses my purpose? Examples: demand, plead, remind, support

Most important is that students strongly indicated in May that focusing and planning their writing made it easier to do and improved it.

Add a Metacognitive Dimension to Familiar Language Arts Practice

One method for teachers to model is to engage students in a structured approach, such as guided reading. Although guided reading is not new, it has been emphasized in teachers' professional development over the past few years. As you review the following description of guided reading, consider how the method can emphasize metacognition.

Guided reading

Guided reading is a procedure that involves small groups in working through a three-part structure: before, during, and after reading. It allows teachers to model reading strategies and to coach students in their reading. The goal of guided reading is to foster effective independent reading by the students. Two critical questions for teachers are these: How will students be grouped? Which text will be selected for the group? Although it is usually most effective to group readers of similar ability together, as part of artful practice, teachers sometimes decide that a student may benefit from the modelling of a more accomplished reader.

BEFORE READING

• Brainstorm to establish prior knowledge.
• Make predictions, for example, about setting or content.
• Consider a focus question (purpose for reading).
• Focus on important vocabulary.

DURING READING

• As students read independently, observe them for engagement, perseverance, and active use of reading strategies.

AFTER READING

• Discuss the passage with an emphasis on returning to the text to confirm interpretation.
• Discuss responses to the focus question.
• Consider predictions and vocabulary.

   If the approach to guided reading is reduced to a formula to get the right answers, it is not metacognitive; however, if the process is open to possibilities beyond the formula and invites self-regulation, it becomes metacognitive. Many students will benefit from an exploration of strategies beyond prediction. To stress metacognition in guided reading, invite students to describe options for processing an unfamiliar text rather than to simply follow directions. In other words, ask, "What do you do when something doesn't make sense in your reading?" or "What do you do so that your reading makes sense?"

   The key question is "How can we read this text so that you will understand it?" As students articulate options and strategies without the teacher's direction, they show that they are becoming metacognitive. The question "From today's work, what did you learn about yourself as a reader?" adds a metacognitive dimension to the After Reading stage of guided reading. Students will come to understand that their learning about themselves is different from that of other students.

Close reading

An emphasis on metacognition can foster close, attentive reading of text, something that students may find challenging. When students struggle to make sense of a text, focus on metacognitive use of strategies is timely. *What have I tried? What else could I try?*

Here are several possible strategies for strengthening ability to do close reading:

• Students might use their own words to note their reading purpose.
• If students own the book or are working with photocopied pages, they might highlight text and make marginal notes.
• A popular option for many students is to use Post-it notes with materials that they are not allowed to mark on.
• Many students read more closely when they employ a graphic organizer. (See example.)

In all of these cases, students should be challenged to identify the strategy that works best for them with a particular text.

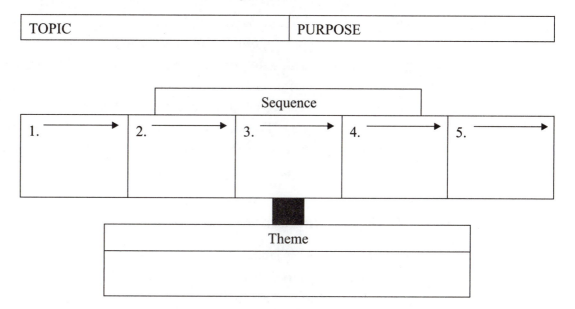

When students are required to answer questions about a text, they can also make metacognitive choices. Some students benefit from reading the questions before they read the text. Other students come to learn that they do better by reading the text before they review the questions. Another rich possibility to encourage metacognitive close reading is to have students return to passages that they have misinterpreted or have interpreted incompletely. Challenge students to note the details that caused them to interpret the text as they did and the details that would now cause them to interpret the text differently.

A Junior High student employed close reading of the text to correct his misinterpretation of a line from "The Parable of the Prodigal Son" from the biblical book of Luke. The line reads: "And he arose and came to his father. But when he was yet a great way off, his father had compassion, and ran and fell on his neck, and kissed him." In discussion, the student revealed that he thought that the old man fell on the ground—part of the problem is the text's unclear pronoun reference for "his." By checking the detail about the kiss, the student concluded that the father kissed his son on the neck and did not injure his own neck by falling to the ground.

You might also have students identify passages that resonate with personal experience and then talk or write about the personal significance of a selected passage. All of this helps students understand themselves as readers and as persons.

Reading surveys

A reading survey form can also promote understanding. When a survey form such as the one on page 35 is used throughout the school year, students can note changes in their reading preferences. In one revealing instance, in a beginning-of-the-year survey, a Grade 10 student wrote: "I enjoy reading books that relate to our ways of living. Some people might think my favourite books are dirty books. But they are good books that deal with problems we have to face—drugs, sex, etc. I like books I can get involved with." The student then listed a few contemporary, escapist titles. In the student's year-end entry, she noted that her favorite title for the year was *The Merchant of Venice*. "The story kept me interested. It helped me understand the meaning of true love and shallow love." This time her metacognitive insight about preferences relates to a text of greater literary merit than her earlier choices.

Wordsplash and other strategies

Metacognition helps students deal with unfamiliar vocabulary, too. Students who groan when they are instructed to look up unfamiliar vocabulary in a dictionary might benefit from an exploration of strategies for learning unfamiliar words. The more strategies that students know, the better they can choose to understand challenging vocabulary in a specific text.

Checking dictionaries, checking context, and looking at prefixes and suffixes are the most familiar strategies for learning vocabulary, but many students prefer one called Wordsplash. The teacher displays selected words randomly at angles on an overhead transparency or chart. Students predict the relationship between the words and the text they are reading; later, they check the accuracy of their predictions. Alternatively, students create a wordsplash of key words after the

MY CURRENT READING FOR PLEASURE SURVEY

Name_____ Date_____

1. My favorite kind of reading materials (magazines, newspapers, poetry books, etc.) is

   _____

   _____

2. I am likely to reread material that

   _____

   _____

3. My favorite place for reading is

   _____

   _____

4. My favorite time for reading is

   _____

   _____

5. The material I am likely to read aloud is

   _____

   _____

6. My favorite author is

   _____

   _____

7. The kind of reading that I am likely to share with others is

   _____

   _____

8. I am likely to finish a book that

   _____

   _____

9. I am unlikely to finish a book that

   _____

   _____

reading of a text. Once again, the metacognitive question is *What vocabulary strategy will work most effectively for me with this particular text?*

Small-group work presents another opportunity for dynamic, metacognitive questioning. In planning group work, teachers and students could usefully reflect on the task, considering what each group is expected to achieve. They could then consider many possibilities. Would assignment of roles be helpful? Would a particular approach, such as Think-Pair-Share or Jigsaw, be appropriate? With Think-Pair-Share, students think on their own before discussing ideas with a partner or group and sharing with the class. Jigsaw breaks up a task, giving each group member a specific assignment. Students meet with other students from other groups with the identical assignment. Following their work in these "expert" groups, students return to their "home" groups to share their work. Would a fishbowl approach in which a group of students observes another group complete a task be helpful? . . . Students will probably work more productively in groups when they help make the decision about how the group will do the task at hand.

Students should always think about ways to use their strengths as learners whether they enjoy the tasks given or not. The range of activities typically found within a language arts program invites students to learn about themselves as learners. In the course of a year, students will likely create collages, dramatize text, present readers' theatre, analyze song lyrics, speak formally and informally, and work as peer editors. They may take part in such approaches as literature circles, in which they contribute according to an assigned role, such as director for the group; illustrator of the text; passagist, the student responsible for looking at selected passages; and connector, the student who connects the text to movies, books, cartoons, news stories, and personal experiences. Throughout these approaches, encourage students to note their favorite activities and preferred roles. Doing so helps them understand their learning preferences and furthers metacognition.

You foster metacognition when you help students recognize when they can use their strengths as learners to complete language arts tasks. Most, but not all language arts work focuses on verbal ability, but some students are stronger in other areas. Why not encourage visual learners, auditory learners, and kinesthetic learners to employ their strengths to improve their verbal skills? For example, if the task is to show how one can use figures of speech to enhance communication, visual learners could examine and create cartoons, illustrations, or displays focused on figurative language; auditory learners could examine and create songs or tape-recorded stories focused on figurative language; and kinesthetic learners could dramatize forms of irony—dramatic, situational, and verbal. This learning should be helpful when students are required to assess figures of speech in poems or print stories.

A chart such as the following should help and encourage you to see different options for your students. Students could relate preferred ways of learning to tasks and curriculum expectations.

Learning Task _____

_____

Expectations/Outcomes Focus _____

_____

Options for Visual Learners	Options for Kinesthetic Learners	Options for Auditory Learners

In keeping with the current interest in differentiated instruction, you would probably want to fill in all columns. This excerpt from *Programming for Students with Special Needs* identifies a range of teaching activities that are appropriate for all visual, kinesthetic, and auditory learners:

Visual	Kinesthetic	Auditory
• Videos • Mind mapping • Painting • Timelines • Diagrams • Filmstrips • Overhead transparencies • Slides, charts, graphs, maps, pictures • Displays • Computer graphics • Visual clues for verbal directions • Exhibits • Note-taking • Models • Microscopes	• Labs • Creative movement • Dioramas • Dramatization • Experiments • Puppetry • Demonstrating • Constructing • Collecting • Games, puzzles • Manipulatives • Field trips • Drawing • Mime	• Panel discussions • Class discussions • Oral directions • Story telling • Direct instruction • Choral reading • Debates • Tape recordings • Interviews • Music • Reader's theatre • Lectures • Songs • Reading aloud

Source: *Programming for Students with Special Needs*, Book 6. Edmonton, AB: Alberta Education. Page LD.95.

The following chart lists several familiar language arts learning activities and suggests ways in which these activities can be given a metacognitive dimension. See whether you can add to the list of alternatives.

Task	Metacognitive Dimension
• Students answer assigned questions about a text.	• Students consider how they answer questions effectively. Does a co-operative learning strategy, such as Think-Pair-Share, work effectively? Do strategies such as using Post-it notes to mark relevant sections of text help?
• Teachers present students with an acronym to guide responses to reading. For example: EVOKER E **Explore** the text by reading it all for general understanding. V Look up unfamiliar **vocabulary**. O Read **orally** the sections that cause difficulty. K Look for **key** ideas. E **Evaluate** the text by answering the who, what, when, where, why and how questions. R **Recap** the information extracted from the above steps.	• After students critically examine the acronym for its fit with the task at hand, they suggest additions, deletions, and modifications to approaches.
• Students explore their thinking and learning by completing a journal entry.	• Students explore alternatives for journal writing, perhaps engaging in different kinds of thinking (comments, questions, predictions, likes/dislikes, connections, examples, doubts, developing understanding) and considering whether representational forms, such as sketches, would improve journals.
• Teachers ask students to brainstorm what they already know about a literary form, such as dramatic monologue.	• Students choose from alternatives to brainstorming, for example, use of graphic organizers, creation of charts or artistic representations of literary forms.
• Teachers present students with a visual form to assist organization of thoughts. For example: a Venn diagram or a character map.	• Students suggest alternatives to these graphic organizers and choose forms that work most effectively for them individually.

Task	Metacognitive Dimension
• Teachers ask students to work in a group to complete a task.	• Students review the task, options for completing the task, and possible assignments.
• Students engage in peer editing.	• Writers identify criteria, including criteria related to personal writing goals, and invite feedback.

Recognizing Performance Assessment in Language Arts

Chapter 1 argued that performance assessment is increasingly important in most academic disciplines. The greater attention that representing and oral language are receiving guarantees this for language arts. Representations and oral language performance require performance assessment as does all writing completed by students. Reading, listening, and viewing are also increasingly seen as language arts suited to performance assessment rather than pre-specified response. Once teachers expect students to compose their interpretations of oral, print, and media text and to support their interpretations with textual evidence, performance assessment is required. The same holds true when students perform or debate a text or when they transform print text into a media text.

Like teachers in other disciplines, language arts teachers need to emphasize three program features so that students will succeed in performance assessments:

1. Student self-assessment and peer-assessment with criteria appropriate to the performance tasks;
2. Assessment with rubrics appropriate to the performance task;
3. Student work with exemplars of performances related to the performance task.

Each of these three assessment program features can and should be metacognitive for learners. For instance, when students engage in self-assessment or peer-assessment with specific criteria appropriate for the task at hand, you can invite them to include a criterion related to a personal learning goal. In a writing assignment, a student who tends to produce wordy and clumsy sentences might choose the criterion of conciseness as a focus. Doing this would be a metacognitive act.

As suggested in Chapter 1, self-assessment is also promoted when students regularly note their learning goals and goals achieved. Students can keep their own records under two columns. This record keeping signals that students are taking ownership of their own learning.

Portfolio approaches also reflect that students are taking ownership of their learning. Students select their best work, explain their choices, and set goals for future work. Although many teachers will connect goal setting with writing, goals related to reading, listening, speaking, viewing, and representing should not be overlooked.

The increasing use of rubrics for a variety of language arts performance clearly reflects a growing emphasis on performance assessment.

Assessment rubrics can foster metacognition. One method is to encourage students to help develop a rubric for the task at hand. Another possibility is for students to suggest additions, deletions, and modifications to criteria on a rubric from a prescribed resource or another source. Rubrics created for an entire country, province, or state often do not fit the assignments completed by a particular group of students. Therefore, involving students in revising published rubrics helps them internalize the requirements of the particular assignment.

Language arts teachers recognize that exemplars of writing, representations, audiotapes, and videotapes should be collected. They can also make students' work with exemplars metacognitive. Students may use exemplars to describe features of a successful performance for a given task. Or, they may work with two exemplars of varying quality and suggest which is superior and why.

Exemplars, whose use is steadily increasing, can also be employed to illustrate metacognitive learning. The following writing sample illustrates metacognition in one student's self-assessment. The Grade 7 class had been focusing on features of effective stories: writing interesting introductions, showing rather than telling, employing precise vocabulary, and demonstrating varied sentence structure. Students used Post-it notes and pencilled arrows to indicate these features in their own texts. Such self-assessment is metacognitive in that the students helped to generate the criteria. More significant evidence of metacognition is that each student used a Post-it note to indicate achievement of a personal writing goal. Ironically, in the sample that appears on page 41, the student has not yet mastered the correct apostrophe form for plural possession (this goal could be revisited in the next assignment). Teachers who employ exemplars like this are showing rather than telling about a feature in the context of a student's composition. Use of the notes demonstrates a metacognitive process to revise writing.

Refocusing Familiar Practice

Attention to metacognition *refines*, rather than supplants familiar teaching practice. All the practices described in this chapter are familiar to language arts teachers: reading and writing processes; K-W-L; guided reading, close-reading strategies; use of graphic organizers; vocabulary building strategies; learning in groups; oral

DISAPPOINTMENT

My most precise words.

Joan was walking in front of her parent's summer home collecting seashells. She had collected about everything that had caught her eye, when, while walking back, she stumbled upon an old rusty bottle, it seemed to have something in it so she went for a closer look.

Correct use of the apostrophe—my personal goal.

Introduction creates interest.

She had been right in her judging—there was a note inside. She took the bottle home, cracked it open and immediately began reading:

> "To whomever finds this, my name is Judy. I'm 13 and looking for a pen-pal."

The note went on listing hobbies, favorite things, grade and other things describing her. Most of the note had been rubbed out, but that didn't stop Joan; she pulled out a piece of paper and began writing. She then sent it to the address indicated. Now all she had to do was wait.

The letter had been a long awaited item, and when it arrived it was received with enthusiasm and open arms. It read:

> "Dear Joan,
> It was very nice of you to write back, but I am sorry to say that I wrote that note at least 17 years ago. I'm sorry if I disappointed you.
>
> Judy"

A saddened look came over Joan's face. She was disappointed, upset, and angry most of all.

A sentence which begins with something other than the subject.

She sat down and began writing down her name, address and other information. Then, taking one of her father's wine bottles, she stuck the note inside. She then walked out to the beach and threw the bottle as far as she could and hoped that someone would go through the same thing.

My best showing not telling.

The year was 2003 A.D. Chris was swimming in the inter-galactic sea pit when she felt something under her foot. It was an antique-looking wine bottle . . .

Source: *Performance Assessment: Encouraging Student Success and Establishing Standards*. English Language Arts Program of Studies K–9 Orientation: Session 4. Series prepared for Alberta Regional Consortium.

language, viewing, and representing activities; differentiated instruction; answering questions about text; use of acronyms to guide responses; journaling; learning about literary form; peer editing; student self-assessment and goal setting; and work with rubrics and exemplars. These methods work better when language arts students become more and more reflective, independent, and responsible, in other words, more metacognitive.

3 Mathematics: A Way to Deepen Understanding

Determining how metacognition manifests itself in the teaching and learning of mathematics depends on your own view of mathematical learning. What does understanding mathematics mean to you? How do you know when your students understand? How do you expect your students to communicate their mathematical understanding?

It seems obvious that mathematics should make sense to students and that understanding should be the most fundamental goal of mathematics instruction. The issue of students learning mathematics meaningfully, or with understanding, has been a recurring theme for those concerned with mathematics education throughout the past decades; nonetheless, learning mathematics *without* understanding has been a common outcome of school mathematics instruction. Consider this seventh grade student's definition of mathematics that appears in a National Council of Supervisors of Mathematics publication: "Math is moving numbers around on paper to get the answer the teacher has" (NCSM 1997, I-15). In recalling your own experiences with learning mathematics, what classroom memories come to mind? Were you encouraged or ever required to reflect on your own thinking? Do you feel that, as a result of all your experiences with learning mathematics, mathematical thinking is one of your strengths? Quite possibly not.

Learning Skills with Understanding

Many adults recall learning mathematics as a generally unpleasant experience—dull, difficult, and often confusing. They remember working on problems alone, completing pages and pages of practice on the same kind of arithmetic, having to memorize seemingly endless and unrelated facts, procedures, definitions, and formulas, and feeling quite uncomfortable in tackling a unique or difficult problem.

Now consider your own students. Have you ever had students who are adept at memorizing facts and procedures, but then act frustrated and unhappy when confronted with problems that don't look like the ones they are used to solving? Do you often come across students who can find common denominators to add two fractions, such as $\frac{5}{6}$ and $\frac{7}{8}$, but don't know just by looking at these fractions that the sum will be a little less than 2?

The myth that students learn by remembering what they are taught continues to permeate mathematics instruction. As long as learning mathematics is seen as mastering a set of basic skills, metacognition will play a minor role in mathematics instruction—and understanding mathematics will continue to elude far too many students. However, more educators are coming to value metacognitive activity as well as to develop ways to foster it. Helping children to understand their own thinking and to express it clearly to others should be a basic tenet of the mathematics curriculum.

In recent years, societal expectations for school mathematics and the vision that mathematics educators espouse for the teaching and learning of mathematics have changed significantly. The accelerating rate of change in our society requires that students now need to learn how to learn, make their world understandable, and be confident in their abilities to do this. Most would agree that the need to truly understand and be able to use mathematics in everyday life and in the workplace has never been greater. Reform efforts in mathematics education have maintained a steady focus on understanding, and there is a tremendous thrust towards ensuring that developing "deep," conceptual understanding and reflective habits of mind—both hallmarks of metacognition—penetrates all mathematical learning. This thrust does not mean ignoring skills instruction. Rather, in order to learn skills so that they are remembered when needed, can be applied flexibly, and can be adjusted to solve new problems, skills must be learned with understanding.

Learning skills with a metacognitive mindset provides an ideal way of developing understanding. In fact, in *Principles and Standards for School Mathematics*, a reform document of the National Council of Teachers of Mathematics (NCTM), reflection and communication are highlighted as intertwined processes that are essential in mathematics learning.

Reflection occurs when you consciously think about an experience. Thoughtful questions posed by a teacher or classmates can cause students to re-examine their thinking. For example, questions such as these suggested in *Professional Standards for Teaching Mathematics* help students work together to make sense of mathematics:

- Does anyone have the same answer, but a different way to explain it?
- Can you convince the rest of us that that makes sense?

Questions such as

- Why do you think that?
- Why is that true?
- Does that make sense?
- Can you draw a picture or use materials to represent that?
- How did you decide your answer was right?

stimulate students to rely more on themselves to determine whether something is mathematically correct and less on the teacher as the sole authority.

Questions such as these help students learn to reason mathematically:

- Does that always work?
- Can you think of a counter example?
- How could you prove that?

Questions such as

- What would happen if …?
- Do you see a pattern?
- Can you predict the next one? What about the last one?
- What is alike and what is different about your method of solution and hers?

encourage students to conjecture and solve problems (NCTM 1991, 3–4).

Reflection means turning ideas over in your head, considering things from different points of view, stepping back to look at things once again, and consciously thinking about what you are doing and why you are doing it.

Communication, which involves talking, listening, writing, demonstrating, observing, and more, means sharing thoughts with others and listening to others' ideas, as well as communicating with oneself. Communication permits us to challenge each other's ideas and ask for clarification and further explanation, all of which encourages us to think more deeply about our own ideas.

Reviewing Curriculum Change in Mathematics Education

Most current, outcomes-based mathematics curricula have explicitly incorporated the process standards featured in *Principles and Standards for School Mathematics*. These interrelated standards—problem solving, reasoning, communication, connections, and representation—serve to highlight ways of acquiring and using content knowledge. They also clearly provide the metacognitive dimension needed to help develop deep mathematical understanding.

Problem solving

Two decades ago, in its *Agenda for Action*, the National Council of Teachers of Mathematics proposed that problem solving be the focus of mathematics instruction. The intent of this goal was for teachers to take a problem-solving, or thinking, approach to the teaching and learning of mathematics. The goal acknowledged that effective problem solvers exhibit metacognitive behavior by constantly monitoring, or self-assessing, their progress and adjusting what they are doing. George Polya's (1957) description of problem-solving activity (understanding, planning, carrying out the plan, and looking back) was frequently identified as the model for instruction. The four phases served as a framework for identifying distinct heuristic processes that could foster successful problem solving. Strategies such as using manipulative materials, drawing diagrams, looking for patterns, listing all possibilities, trying special values or cases, working backward, guessing and checking, and creating a simpler problem were specifically modelled and taught.

Unfortunately, in the predominantly "teach-then-solve" paradigm that persists in our culture, the intent of this goal has all too often been misinterpreted. Rather than develop reflective habits of mind that penetrate all mathematical learning, problem solving often becomes a discrete and frequently disliked topic of mathematics instruction.

Current mathematics curricula, however, insist that problem solving is an integral part of *all* mathematics learning. They thereby reflect a more metacognitive approach to mathematics instruction. For example, as stated in the Western Canadian Protocol and Alberta Program of Studies (1996),

> Problem solving is to be employed throughout all of mathematics and should be embedded throughout all of the strands.

> Problem solving provides an opportunity for students to be active in constructing mathematical meaning, to learn problem-solving strategies, to practise a variety of concepts and skills in a meaningful context, and to communicate mathematical ideas (p. 8).

In other words, solving problems is not only a goal of learning mathematics, but is also a major means of doing so. Problem solving places the focus of students' attention on ideas and sense making. When teachers engage students in carefully selected tasks or activities that are problematic and require thought, teachers can begin with the mathematical ideas that children already have and will use to create new ones. Children learn mathematics by doing mathematics when problem solving is intrinsic to the instructional program.

Teaching mathematics through problem solving, by structuring lessons to promote reflective thought, does not imply negating or de-emphasizing basic skills or computational procedures. Rather, research increasingly shows that most, if not all, important mathematical concepts, procedures, and skills can most effectively be taught through problem solving. For example, the best way in which children construct operation meanings is by solving word problems. Clear distinctions among the different types of addition, subtraction, multiplication, and division problems can be made only through the context of meaningful situations. Otherwise, the conceptual understandings of these operations remain superficial, one-dimensional, and incomplete.

Note the various interpretations illustrated in the following simple situations. These can all be represented with subtraction equations, but are routinely described as "take aways" by children.

- Megan had 17 dollars in her peanut butter jar, but took out ten dollars to help pay for a birthday present for her dad. How much money is left in Megan's jar?
(Take away: $17 - 10 = 7$)
- Four people chose chocolate milk for lunch, and seven chose juice. How many more chose juice than milk?
(Comparison, or using one-to-one correspondence: $7 - 4 = 3$)
- If I cover half this domino, you will see only four dots. Altogether, the domino has ten dots. How many dots on the domino are covered?
(Missing addend: $4 + \Box = 10$, or $10 - 4 = 6$)

Word problems provide essential opportunities for examining diverse meanings for each operation. If approached inquiringly, they allow children to use their own solution methods and to justify their solutions.

Problem solving provides a consistent, metacognitive context for learning and applying mathematics. It enables a teacher to establish a classroom climate that clearly encourages and supports problem-solving efforts, and where students, young as well as older, learn to value the *process* of solving problems as much as they value the solutions. A problem-solving approach to instruction continually nurtures the reflective habits of mind necessary for lifelong learning. It also helps students develop their abilities to understand and apply a variety of appropriate strategies.

Consider the following coin problem:

With one quarter, two dimes, five nickels, and twenty-five pennies, how many different ways can you make 25 cents?

Here, a basic knowledge of the value of pennies, nickels, dimes, and quarters is required, as well as some understanding of addition. Students could use real coins to act out or demonstrate different solutions to the problem. Using a trial-and-error strategy, they could consider and find some solutions that may not be immediately obvious to them. If challenged to identify all the possible ways, they could make an organized list or table of coin combinations (like the one shown) to verify that each of their answers satisfies the conditions of the problem and that they have identified all the possibilities. Furthermore, students could extend the problem-solving experience by posing their own variations of the problem.

Coin Problem

Quarter	Dimes	Nickels	Pennies	Total 25 cents
1 (25)	0	0	0	25
0	2 (20)	1 (5)	0	20 + 5 = 25
0	2 (20)	0	5	20 + 5 = 25
0	1 (10)	3 (15)	0	10 + 15 = 25
0	1 (10)	2 (10)	5	10 + 10 + 5 = 25
0	1 (10)	1 (5)	10	10 + 5 + 10 = 25
0	1 (10)	0	15	10 + 15 = 25
0	0	5 (25)	0	25
0	0	4 (20)	5	20 + 5 = 25
0	0	3 (15)	10	15 + 10 = 25
0	0	2 (10)	15	10 + 15 = 25
0	0	1 (5)	20	5 + 20 = 25
0	0	0	25	25

Identifying and selecting mathematical problems that promote a metacognitive approach to teaching and learning is a critical teacher responsibility. A wide range of materials exists from which teachers can choose. However, good tasks help students understand concepts and skills in a way that also fosters their ability to think mathematically and to become independent learners. Consider these key questions in selecting a worthwhile task:

• Does the problem involve work with significant mathematical ideas and relationships?
• Does it elicit higher-level thinking?
• Does it require students to do the thinking?
• Does it provide purpose?
  – Does the task lead students to consider important mathematical ideas that reach beyond the solution?

- Is the problem interesting to a wide range of students?
- Does the problem allow for multiple solution paths?
  - Are there different ways into this problem? Students with different strengths, needs, and experiences should be able to engage with some aspects of the problem.
  - Do the constraints of the problem provide enough direction and structure without overly restricting the ways in which students might think about the problem?
- Are manipulatives seen as a tool, not a mandate?
- Are students asked to reflect on and communicate their thinking and work?

Reasoning

As this definition from *Supporting Improvement in Mathematics Education* conveys, mathematics is more than a collection of concepts, skills, and procedures.

> From the Greek, *to learn*. It is the study of relationships (between numbers, between shapes), a search for pattern and order, an attempt to make sense of the world. This study involves making connections, seeing patterns, seeing order, using logic, making predictions, creating hypotheses, proving them, solving problems. (I-14)

Mathematics is reasoning. Being able to reason, to explain and to justify your thinking, is a critical component of problem solving and essential to understanding mathematics. Without reasoning, the logical thinking that helps us to determine if and why our answers make sense, mathematics is reduced to mindless skills.

However, mathematical reasoning cannot develop in isolation. Too many children come to view mathematics as a rigid set of rules governed by standards of accuracy, speed, and memory. As young children, though, they are curious and engage in mathematical activity naturally, sorting objects, discovering patterns, and making conjectures based on observation. Little by little, their view of mathematics shifts. They move from enthusiasm to apprehension, and from confidence to fear. The ability to reason is a process that must be patiently nurtured throughout the grades. It grows out of many experiences that convince children that mathematics makes sense.

A metacognitive approach to mathematics instruction insists that if students are to learn to rely on their own mathematical reasoning, they need encouragement to justify their solutions, thinking processes, and conjectures in a variety of ways. For example, they could use physical models, pictures, known facts, and properties. They must also be encouraged to explain their reasoning in their own words. Having to justify their responses forces students to think reflectively.

All students need to develop the habit of providing a rationale as an integral part of an answer. The consistent use of such oral and written prompts as the following conveys to students the importance of reflective thinking, as well as the idea that the reasons for their answers are at least as important as the answers themselves.

- Explain how you got your answer.
- Show your work.
- Tell why you think so.
- What is the relationship between this problem and others we have done?

J. Higgins, in an article in *Arithmetic Teacher*, makes these insightful comments: "As teachers, we get what we ask for. If we ask only for simple numerical answers, children will value only procedures and computational tasks. But, if we ask for discussion, explanation, and elaboration; and if we reward these kinds of answers, then children will value understanding and meaning" (1988, 2).

It is crucial to note that reasoning does not always lead to correct results. Sometimes reasoning, even very careful reasoning, is flawed. In order to make mathematical reasoning the true focus in mathematics classrooms, we must expect to encounter and examine flawed reasoning often. Students must develop the view that it is commonplace to analyze and rethink, to poke at theories and test them thoroughly, to face one's own and others' questions, and to experience what it is like to think through reasoning that did not work. Equally important, flawed reasoning often reveals important mathematical issues that all students need to think through.

Communication

This process standard highlights the ability to talk about, write about, describe, and explain mathematical ideas. It is inextricably tied to problem solving and reasoning, and facilitates a metacognitive approach to learning mathematics. As students' mathematical language develops, so does their ability to reflect on, reason about, and solve problems. Furthermore, problem-solving situations provide a setting for the development and extension of communication skills and reasoning ability.

Mathematics is often thought of and expressed in symbols. As a result, key communication skills, such as representing, talking, listening, writing, and reading, are not always recognized as an important part of teaching and learning mathematics. Yet no better way exists for wrestling with an idea than to attempt to articulate it to others. Interacting with classmates helps students construct knowledge, learn other ways to think about ideas, and clarify their own thinking. However, questions that limit answers to recitation of a single number, a simple yes or no, or a memorized procedure do not teach students the communication skills they need. They also fail to give teachers any rich information from which they can make sound instructional decisions. On the other hand, thoughtful questions can provoke students to re-examine their reasoning and organize and record their thinking.

Writing in mathematics, which may take many forms, also helps students to consolidate their thinking. It requires them to reflect on their work, often more thoroughly and systematically, and to clarify their thoughts about ideas developed in a lesson. See how an assignment which required Grade 3 students to consider and show two different ways to do the addition below yielded powerful insights into one child's understanding.

$$
\begin{array}{r}
99 \\
199 \\
+\ \underline{299} \\
\end{array}
$$

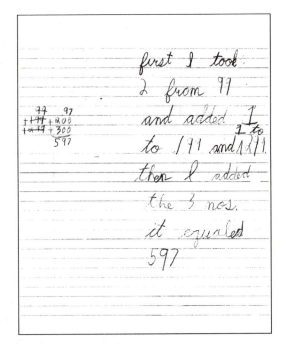

Neither of the procedures described by the student reflects the traditional algorithm most adults would associate with the addition. The first solution demonstrates a solid understanding of place value, particularly, representing "27 tens" as 270, which facilitates working from left to right. The second solution is constructive, allowing the child to conveniently decrease the first number by 2 and increase each of the others by 1 to keep the numbers in balance. Both solutions eliminated the need for "regrouping" or "carrying," a dominant and sometimes troublesome feature of the traditional algorithm.

In the next example, the student demonstrates a solution process that eliminates the need to "carry" and represents the thinking involved in three distinct modes—symbolically, using numbers; pictorially, representing base ten materials; and in writing.

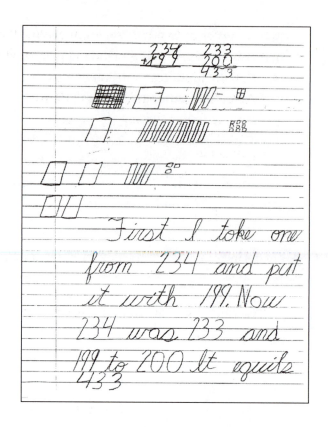

First I toke one from 234 and put it with 199. Now 234 was 233 and 199 to 200. It equils 433

It is important to keep in mind that students' thinking or problem-solving abilities and their communication skills may not always be at the same level. Sometimes, what first appears as an incorrect response may be, in fact, an inability to communicate.

Emphasizing communication in a mathematics class fosters a metacognitive approach to mathematics teaching and learning. It does so by shifting the classroom from an environment in which students depend totally on the teacher to one in which they assume more responsibility for validating their own thinking. Actively engaging students in small-group work and large-group discussions, as well as individual assignments, creates an environment in which students can practise and refine their growing ability to communicate mathematical thought processes and strategies. Small groups provide varying opportunities for students to ask questions, discuss ideas, make mistakes, learn to listen to others' ideas, offer constructive criticism, and summarize their discoveries in writing. Whole-class discussions enable students to pool and evaluate ideas, record and summarize collected data, share and compare solution strategies, hypothesize, and construct conclusions. As with each of the other process standards, mathematical expression is part of the process of actively doing mathematics, not an end in itself. Students who have ongoing opportunities, encouragement, and support for speaking, writing, reading, and listening in mathematics classes communicate to learn mathematics and learn to communicate mathematically.

Another significant curriculum change that reflects a metacognitive approach to mathematics instruction is the manner in which specific learner outcomes are stated. Consider these four outcomes that appear in the Western Canadian Protocol and Alberta Program of Studies (1996):

Justify the choice of method for addition and subtraction, using:
- estimation strategies
- mental mathematics strategies
- manipulatives
- algorithms
- calculator

[Communication, Problem Solving, Reasoning, Technology]

Grade 3 (p. 119)

Describe how a pattern grows, using everyday language in spoken and written form.
[Communication, Connections]

Grade 5 (p. 168)

Explain, demonstrate and use proportion in solving problems.
[Communication, Problem Solving, Visualization]

Grade 7 (p. 222)

Explain, in more than one way, why the sum of the measures of the angles of a triangle is 180°. [Communication, Reasoning, Technology]

Grade 7 (p. 232)

As outcomes, these four examples identify what students are expected to know and be able to do, but also demand a much deeper understanding of the content being referenced. They reflect that it is now a clear expectation that students are able to demonstrate their abilities to reason, communicate, and solve problems using a variety of strategies.

Establishing a Learning Environment for Mathematical Thinking

Students' understanding of mathematics, as well as their confidence in and disposition towards mathematics, is shaped by the teaching they encounter and the experiences that classroom teachers provide. Teachers play a critical role in establishing a metacognitive learning environment. Certainly there is no one "right way" to teach. However, for metacognition to flourish in mathematics classrooms, teachers need to engage in reflective practice, continuous self-improvement, and effective mathematics teaching.

Effective mathematics teachers draw upon a rich knowledge base that includes several different kinds of mathematical knowledge. They know and understand the big ideas of mathematics and can represent mathematics as a coherent and connected discipline; they also have a deep, flexible knowledge about curriculum goals and about the important ideas central to their grade level. Teachers need to understand the different representations of a mathematical idea, the relative strengths and weaknesses of each, and how they are related to one another. They need to be able to identify the ideas with which students often have difficulty, as well as ways to help bridge common misunderstandings. Equally important though, they must understand the thinking processes and strategies appropriate for learning and using mathematical content, and be able to match them to effective teaching strategies.

Teachers are responsible for creating a learning environment where mathematical thinking is the norm. Beyond the physical setting of desks, displays, and materials, the classroom environment communicates subtle messages about what is valued in learning mathematics. Key components of a learning environment in which serious mathematical thinking can occur include the following:

• a genuine respect for everyone's ideas and varying methods
• a valuing of reason and sense-making
• an appreciation for mistakes as "learning sites"

In such a learning environment all students can learn to think mathematically.

Reconsidering the Nature of Assessment

Traditionally, mathematics teachers have assessed academic progress through the use of paper-and-pencil tools, such as multiple-choice and short-answer tests. The assumption has generally been that correct answers mean mastery and wrong answers suggest learning deficiencies. But as mathematics teaching becomes more diverse, including an emphasis on thinking and communication, teachers need to use multiple forms of assessment. By doing so they will best be able to make valid inferences about students' progress.

What are we willing to accept as evidence of students' understanding?

Obviously, only some forms of assessment can promote and reflect metacognitive processes in mathematics learning. As in each of the other subject areas, various forms of performance assessment provide students the best opportunities to demonstrate what they know and can do, and to do their own organizing and thinking. Performance assessments help students understand that mathematics is not a set of rules to memorize and follow, but a process that enables people to solve problems. Some performance assessments consist of short tasks, for example, solving problems, responding to writing prompts, or answering open-ended questions; others involve longer student projects or investigations.

All performance assessments can be scored using rubrics. Teachers can design or adapt these for, or with, a particular group of students or a particular mathematical task. A rubric and its accompanying performance indicators should focus the teacher and students on their goals, their total performance on a task (processes, answers, justifications, and extensions), and the possibility to excel. Students need information about what doing good mathematics looks like. They also need to know what the expectations are for acceptable and exceptional performances. One Thinking About My Work rubric, intended for students at the Junior High level, appears on pages 56 and 57 as an example. Such a rubric works equally well for mathematics and science (the focus of the next chapter).

Student self-assessment also promotes metacognition, ownership of learning, and independent thinking. Self-assessment activities may take many forms ranging from problem-solving strategy inventories, self-assessment checklists, attitude inventories and questionnaires to developing class goals and using open-ended writing prompts such as these:

- Complete one or more of the following statements:
  – I learned …
  – I noticed that I …
  – I discovered …
  – I was pleased that I …
- The method of _____ that I am most comfortable with is …
- Describe any places you became "stuck" when working on _____.
  Tell what happened to help you get "unstuck."
- Explain what is most important to understand about _____.

In summary, teachers can promote metacognitive thinking in mathematics. They need to think about mathematics differently—beyond just concepts and skills—change their expectations of students, and reconsider student assessment.

THINKING ABOUT MY WORK RUBRIC
(Developed for Mathematics and Science)

	Problem Solving	Student ✓	Teacher ✓	Communication	Student ✓	Teacher ✓
1 "Don't Understand"	• I did not understand what I was supposed to do.			• I didn't know what to write and what I did write isn't very clear.		
	• I collected some data, but I didn't know how to use it.			• I didn't know how to explain what I wrote.		
	• I couldn't find an answer/ I guessed at the answer.			• Math/science terms, tables, and graphs don't make sense to me so I don't use them.		
2 "Not Quite There"	• I was confused, but I think I figured out a way to do it.			• I had an idea of what I wanted to say, but I had trouble putting it into words.		
	• I didn't collect data/I collected data, but I'm not sure if it is the right information.			• I'm not sure if what I wrote makes sense.		
	• I was able to answer the question, but I can't explain it and I'm not sure that it is correct.			• I find it hard to use the right math/science words. I don't know if my graph and table are right.		
	• I got an answer, but I'm not sure how I got it.			• I don't think that I wrote enough information, but I don't know what else to write.		

	Problem Solving	Student	Teacher	Communication	Student	Teacher
3	• I had a good idea of what I was supposed to do and I was able to figure out a way to do it.			• I was able to provide a mostly clear and logical explanation.		
"I've Got It"	• I collected the data I needed to find the answer.			• I tried to make my answer clear and provide some details.		
	• I found the answer and I was able to explain it fairly well using my results.			• I can use some math/science words, tables, and graphs in my explanation.		
	• My plan worked.					
4	• I knew what information I needed to solve the problem and I knew exactly how to get it.			• I was able to provide a clear and logical explanation.		
"Going Beyond"	• I collected the data that I needed.			• My answer is detailed and easy to follow.		
	• I found the answer and I was able to provide a really complete explanation using my results.			• I can use math/science words, tables, and graphs in my explanation.		
	• My plan worked. Others could repeat it and get the same results.					

4 Science: A Way to Reconstruct Knowledge

Although the term *metacognition* does not receive more than a fleeting nod in science curricular documents or in science education research, *thinking about one's own thinking* is the keystone of the problem-solving and inquiry processes. In teaching and learning the discipline of science, two aspects of metacognition should be recognized:

1. Thinking about my own understandings: *How do I know what I know? What evidence or experience supports my thinking?* (Conceptual Understanding)
2. Thinking about constructing new understandings through problem solving and inquiry: *How will I find out what I want to know? How will I find solutions to the problems and challenges facing me?* (Inquiry, Problem-Solving, and Decision-Making Skills)

Seeking Conceptual Understanding

It is impossible in thirteen years of education (Kindergarten to Grade 12) to teach everything there is to know about science. Instead, science education reform has called for a move to scientific literacy. *Science for Every Student*, published by the Science Council of Canada in 1984, prompted Canadian educators to consider the knowledge, skills, and attitudes that graduating students must take with them in order to apply a reasonable level of science understanding to their daily lives. The National Research Council has defined scientific literacy to mean "that a person can ask, find, or determine answers to questions derived from curiosity about everyday experiences" (1996, 22). This definition begs the question: How do we learn science in such a way as to become discerning enough to "ask, find or determine answers"? One answer is that people who can think metacognitively are able to consider their own understandings and choose appropriate and effective strategies for solving novel problems.

Much research and commentary have been devoted to the notion of conceptual change in science learning. Prior knowledge and skill are the filters through which learners sift all new information. Learners are encouraged to move from naïve understandings of science to those substantiated by evidence. This emphasis presumes that both the teacher and the student must first recognize and acknowledge current understandings in order for the learner to rethink something. How can this be done so as to involve the student in the metacognitive process of asking *What do I know? What evidence or experiences support my understanding?*

Journal articles and teacher manuals outline several strategies ranging from classroom discussion to graphic organizers to meet this requirement. To begin with, the teacher makes a metacognitive choice about the strategy to accomplish a particular task. Through teacher modelling, students gain experience and confidence so that they will be able to make similar choices about the best approach(es) for assessing their own understandings. Below are some of the strategies promoted as useful in determining students' prior knowledge. When and why would each process be employed?

Strategy	Description of the Strategy	Why Use It?
K-W-L	A three-column chart that prompts students to explore what they Know about the topic, what they Want to know, and what they Learned through study and exploration	• Focuses on specific information • Involves the student as an active participant who has responsibility for learning • Serves as a useful communicator of knowledge between student and teacher
Venn diagram	The use of intersecting circles to compare and contrast characteristics of two or more things	• Encourages organization and sorting of information into categories • Helps to determine similarities and differences
Flow chart	A diagrammatic representation of the sequence or flow of processes or events	• Helps organize information in sequence • Helps to illustrate relationships, processes, steps, cycles, timelines, and ordering • Can also show interrelationships and feedback loops

Strategy	Description of the Strategy	Why Use It?
Dichotomous keys or classification tables	A large group of items is divided into successively smaller groups based on similar characteristics. Each group is divided into two smaller groups until at the end, there are only a few items in each group, but they share very similar characteristics.	• Aid in selecting and organizing information related to one key concept • Highlight specific details and relationships • Organize information from the big picture to the details • Promote the skills of observing, comparing, ordering, categorizing, and communicating
Concept map	Diagram that connects concepts or ideas by showing the relationships between the discrete pieces of information	• Helps in generating and organizing ideas • Assists in connecting ideas and indicating interrelationships • Serves as a brainstorming activity • Serves as a diagnostic tool or a way to assess changes in the learner's understandings
Large- or small-group brainstorming	Must be conducted in a risk-free environment in which students are freely able to propose or share ideas that occur to them spontaneously about the topic	• Allows for quick generation of ideas and provides a baseline of understanding for the whole group • Encourages group participation and excitement about the topic
Science learning log (journal)	A notebook used for the purpose of personal reflection on the topic of study. Generally, the teacher will provide the framework or parameters for the response, perhaps in the form of a question.	• Provides opportunities for students to explain and examine their own thinking and that of others in a relatively risk-free environment • Serves as a private communication tool between teacher and student • Highlights personal understandings and questions

Strategy	Description of the Strategy	Why Use It?
Statement of hypothesis	After considering a problem posed and the variables involved, providing a possible answer based on prior knowledge and experience	• Indicates beliefs and reasons for them • Provides an insight into the prior experience and background understanding of the student

If prior knowledge is so critical in the learning of new scientific ideas, so too is the fact that the nature of science is often counter-intuitive. For instance, photosynthesis is usually introduced in the upper elementary grades in simple terms: a plant requires water, air, and sunlight in order to produce its own "food." By the time students have taken high school level biology, they can reproduce the photosynthesis equation complete with the biochemical reactions involved. How is it then that, in the interviews of university graduates that appear on the "Minds of Our Own" videotape, very few were able to make the connection between the unseen carbon dioxide required in photosynthesis and the final mass of the plant itself? Some of those graduates even majored in science. It seems not to make sense that the "invisible" gas could be a major building block of the plant itself. The students' intuition (*something invisible cannot be that important*) and an incomplete understanding of the particle nature of matter (rearrangement of atoms to form new molecules through chemical reaction) stand in the way of grasping the full process of photosynthesis. And so, students leave with the same preconceptions that they entered the learning with: recognizing the importance of water and energy in the photosynthesis reaction because these seem obvious, but overlooking the importance of carbon dioxide.

What do learners do when confronted with evidence or information that conflicts with their prior knowledge? The choices are to

• ignore the new ideas in favor of the more comfortable existing knowledge
• try to incorporate some of the new information into the existing framework of understanding
• grapple with the new concepts, thereby forcing modification, adaptation, or abandonment of the old understanding

Clearly, the last option is the most difficult, but also results in a fuller and deeper understanding of the new information. B. C. Dart and colleagues (1998, 296) identify three stages of this metacognitive process for learners:

1. Recognizing their own ideas and beliefs
2. Evaluating these in terms of what is to be learned and how it is to be learned
3. Deciding whether or not to reconstruct their ideas and beliefs

In order for students to reconstruct their ideas and beliefs, they must see that the accumulated evidence puts their current thinking into question. It is not enough to be told that the evidence exists. Individuals must collect the data and make their own inferences and interpretations. While it is unrealistic to expect that the work of brilliant minds throughout history can be duplicated in the classroom, it is important that students can take part in the process of investigation.

Applying Inquiry, Problem-Solving, and Decision-Making Skills

In the seventeenth century, Francis Bacon forged a new scientific movement of inductive reasoning known as *empiricism* (noted in *A History of Western Society*, 1995). Although already practised by Brahe and Galileo, the idea that "new knowledge had to be pursued through empirical, experimental research" flew in the face of traditional thinking (1995, 597). This experimental approach, it was argued, would allow for independent thinking and not be influenced by any other preconceived notions. Scientific inquiry as a means for gaining new knowledge was born. Science as a discipline, however, did not become part of the school curriculum until the nineteenth century (DeBoer 2000, 583).

Scientific method model

Following the 1957 Sputnik launch by the Soviet Union, "the preferred pedagogy was an inquiry approach, not to develop independence of thought as nineteenth century scientists had argued, but to mirror and thereby appreciate the way scientists themselves did their work" (DeBoer 2000, 587). As the space race began, the pressure was on to produce elite scientists to be symbolic of the struggle between capitalism and communism. This thinking led to the belief that to create a community of scientists, there must be a specific methodology that would exemplify scientific research. The result was the linear, step-by-step model known as the scientific method:

1. State the problem to be solved.
2. Determine the variables (controlled, manipulated, and responding) in the problem.
3. Identify the hypothesis, or best guess solution.

4. List the materials to be used.
5. Provide a step-by-step procedure that can be followed by someone else.
6. List observations in a table, a graph, or statements.
7. State the conclusions or interpretations based on the data.

The steps themselves were derived from the formal protocol required in the communication of scientific research. Such a format is crucial in the reporting, discussion, and peer review that must take place among scientists. Much is good and useful in using the framework; however, the formal steps presented as *the* way for solving *all* problems reduced scientific inquiry to an algorithm rather than recognizing its true creative nature. Students participated in recipe-book experiments in which both teacher and student expected that there would be one way to solve the problem with one clear final result. The textbook or laboratory manual provided the problem, materials list, step-by-step procedure, and even the observation chart. Students simply reproduced the experiment and teachers referred to their guides for the correct or expected answers. Although empirical data were collected and interpreted, the process did not challenge students to consider *why this particular method of problem solving was chosen over another.* The end result, after all, was predetermined. Knowing (memorizing?) the answer, rather than appreciating the process, was the valued outcome.

Skill wheel model

In an effort to provide alternatives to the scientific method for problem solving, another model was proposed to deal with the new STS (Science-Technology-Society) curriculum in the early 1990s. Often referred to as the "skill wheel," the model placed the skills of scientific inquiry, technological problem solving, and decision making into three separate circular frameworks. It allowed one to come and go out of the process and encouraged more creativity from the individual. The model itself was and continues to be very useful in guiding inquiry, problem solving, and decision making. However, this approach, like the scientific method, was marred by the prescriptive nature of predetermining which wheel was to be used when the emphasis of the unit at hand determined it. As soon as learners and teachers presume that only one methodology is "correct," then that becomes the only process that students employ and that instructors accept. Again, a false orthodoxy was created. Students would use the Scientific Inquiry Wheel because they were studying a Nature of Science unit, not because they chose it as the best method for solving the problem at hand. The skills of each wheel became discrete by definition.

Example of three separate skill wheels as might be used in a Nature of Science unit

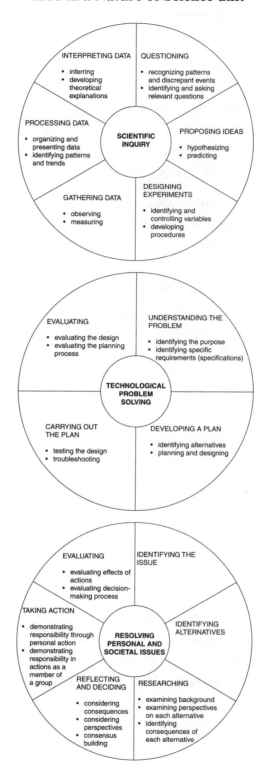

Although the skill wheel model encourages more creativity than the scientific method approach, it falls short of calling for the integration of all skills and thereby making students think about their thinking as is found in outcomes-based curricula.

Source: Alberta Education, 1989

Outcomes-based model

The current outcomes-based science curricula boldly insist on the integration of all skills in each unit of study. Although not stated explicitly, the programs force each individual to become metacognitive. Students and teachers can no longer rely on just one set of skills to solve the challenges posed, but rather must choose the approach(es) best suited to the task.

Recognizing the limitations imposed by linear and prescriptive steps, the Council of Ministers of Education, Canada, identifies four broad skill areas in its *Common Framework of Science Learning Outcomes, K to 12*:

- initiating and planning: These are the skills of questioning, identifying problems, and developing preliminary ideas and plans.
- performing and recording: These are the skills of carrying out a plan of action, which involves gathering evidence by observation and, in most cases, manipulating materials and equipment.
- analyzing and interpreting: These are the skills of examining information and evidence, of processing and presenting data so that it can be interpreted, and of interpreting, evaluating, and applying the results.
- communication and teamwork: In science, as in other areas, communication skills are essential at every stage where ideas are being developed, tested, interpreted, debated, and agreed upon. Teamwork skills are also important, since the development and application of science ideas is a collaborative process both in society and in the classroom. (1994, 12)

The *Common Framework of Science Learning Outcomes* is very clear in stating that there are many ways to solve problems and answer questions and that the skills listed are not intended to "imply a linear sequence or to identify a single set of skills required in each science investigation" (p. 12). It should be noted that this new organization does not abandon the essential skills of science inquiry, problem solving, or decision making, but rather provides an opportunity for the learner to test and choose strategies that are most appropriate to his/her understanding of the problem and the possible solutions. Rather than relying on a set of prescribed approaches, the student is forced to consider such metacognitive questions as *How will I find out what I need to know? How will I find solutions to the problems and challenges facing me?*

To develop *thinkers* rather than *producers of correct answers*, teachers cannot afford to focus on following the steps as determined by someone else. We need to recognize that critical and independent thought is at the centre of the scientific endeavor. To become metacognitive, students must have, at the very least, the opportunities to choose the methods and materials for solving the posed problems.

They also require the time to share, discuss, question, assess, and reflect on their approaches and those of others.

Consider the challenge and question that follow. They provide examples of metacognitive activities. The metacognitive challenge is to determine how to arrive at solutions using current understandings and skills. Sometimes, a learner discovers that more knowledge or different/greater skill is required.

a) Challenge: *Using only the materials provided (50 straws, 25 paper clips, one sheet of paper, 30 cm of masking tape), build the tallest freestanding structure that will support a golf ball above the ground for a minimum of three minutes.*

In order to solve this problem learners, ideally in pairs, must work collaboratively to

- determine their existing knowledge and experience as it relates to structures, forces, and the materials provided for building
- test the materials and make predictions based on these tests
- plan and build or build and plan, constantly refining and adjusting their work (sometimes based on what they may glean from the work of other groups)
- test and assess their own designs and constructions

Students do not need to have these processes outlined for them before exposure to the challenge. They will work through the problem as they see fit. Some will progress in a methodical fashion, while others may stumble through in no particular order. Some may formalize a plan before building; others may "mess around" first and figure out the plan as they go. All will come up with something, even if it doesn't meet all the requirements. Discussion, peer review, and personal reflection allow for the students to learn from one another and for the teacher to assess movement along the understanding and skill continuum. The greatest learning opportunities come from discussion among team members during the building activity and in the explanation of the varying strategies used once the activity is completed.

b) Question: *How do we assess and monitor human impact on a schoolyard eco-system?* Prior to posing this question, students will have explored interactions of biotic and abiotic components of an ecosystem. They will have studied the schoolyard ecosystem and identified the presence of human impact in various areas. In order to answer this question students must

- discuss and reflect upon what they value and need from the schoolyard

- make detailed observations and inferences from the schoolyard relative to its current composition including but not limited to human impact
- work together to identify good questions about the schoolyard that can be investigated with the equipment available and in the time allotted (These questions should be of interest to the students and also meet curriculum requirements.)
- determine appropriate procedures for assessing components of the ecosystem and then monitoring specific aspects so as to fulfill the expectations of the questions they have posed
- conduct the investigations, constantly refining the procedure and/or equipment
- collect and represent data
- follow the procedures for monitoring, recognizing that protocol often exists for the collection and representation of data
- share, discuss, review, reflect upon, and interpret data

This process may include guided discovery, where the teacher establishes the direction of the study, but allows for student choice of procedures, as well as open-ended investigation, where the students have the freedom to identify the questions and the processes of inquiry. In both cases, the students determine what they already know and can do, then determine how they will proceed. The teacher works to facilitate and guide this movement, not to prescribe the "right" steps. The manner in which the students move through the process may indicate their knowledge and skill and help to inform further instruction.

Metacognitive students make choices in the questions they ask and in the methods and materials they use to solve problems. They cannot make choices if they have nothing to choose from. And so it is important that they have opportunities as identified below:

- Students need to witness inquiry, problem-solving, and decision-making processes used by others.
  Think-alouds can move students towards more independent choice of strategies. In a think-aloud, the teacher and students verbalize the thought processes and decision making used in working through a problem. In so doing, others can follow the process and may even suggest alternatives or modifications. The teacher provides examples of a variety of methodologies and encourages students to take the risk of considering other possibilities. The process is dynamic, not limited to a series of predetermined steps in a one-size-fits-all scenario.

- Students should be able to review methods used by others in solving problems and acquiring knowledge.
  The use of science learning logs (journals, field books), debate, discussion, peer

review (pair share) allows the learner to talk about, reflect upon, and weigh possible strategies. In sharing ideas with their peers, the students can evaluate their own thinking against that of others. *What works for me? What works for others? Why?*

Matthew Grade 3.   My Beam Bridge

Instructions:
① Use the notched popcicle sticks to build 2 checkerboard shapes.
② Connect the 2 checkerboards with more notched popcicles. This makes the base for the bridge.
③ Glue regular popcicle sticks on sides, and down the middle of the base. This creates the deck.
④ podgy the deck.

Problems and soultions:
① Knex was not strong enough. I tried popcicle sticks because they are stronger.
② The middle of the bridge was bending. I put support where it was bending.
③ some notches were in the wrong spots. Dad cut more notches in the right spots.

Students often ask, Why do we need to know this? Journaling could be used as a vehicle to answer this ever-present question, to guide the journey, to help students to become more metacognitive and to provide students with a meaningful science education experience, meaningful to them personally (Matovinovic 2000, 7).

- Students need to experience a variety of strategies involved in investigating, testing, experimenting, problem solving, and decision making.
The *Common Framework for Science Learning Outcomes* suggests that as early as the end of Grade 3, students should be able to "demonstrate and describe ways of using materials and tools to help answer science questions and to solve practical problems" (page 35). How will students have the ability to choose materials and methods if they have not first tested and tried a variety of approaches? Guided discovery and open-ended inquiry are two major options. Since school science curricula clearly recognize this metacognitive necessity, they require that students actively use a variety of strategies from the time they first enter school.

- Students benefit from opportunities to evaluate strategies against criteria developed with others.

Following an investigation, trouble-shooting session, challenge, debate, or presentation, it is important to debrief personally or collectively on the different strategies used. The emphasis here is not on the "right answer," but rather on the process. Perhaps there are agreed-upon and specified criteria on which to assess the strategies (for example, strongest, tallest, most efficient, supported by evidence, argument clearly stated). Perhaps the assessment is placed on a continuum based on prior knowledge and skill. Regardless, evaluating strategies demands metacognitive ability and promotes learning.

Determining Effective Science Assessment

As in other subjects, student assessment to meet the requirements of the outcomes-based science curricula must address more than knowledge of factual content. Although acquiring new information is still important, learning science involves much more than the memorization of facts, theories, and laws.

In *Understanding by Design*, Grant Wiggins and Jay McTighe (1998) suggest that teachers themselves become more metacognitive in their planning, instruction, and assessment. They propose that teachers first identify the essential or enduring concepts, skills, and attitudes of a unit and then determine the acceptable evidence for demonstrating understanding of those key elements. This intensive process is best accomplished in collaboration with other educators. Determining the acceptable evidence of understanding (student assessment) should be done prior to planning specific activities or assignments.

Below are several questions based on the students' ability to demonstrate science skills and apply new knowledge. Based on frequent and ongoing experimentation, laboratory and field investigations, and classroom activities, ask yourself each question and then consider the best assessment procedure to determine the students' ability.

GUIDING QUESTION: Are my students able to explain, discuss, debate, and extend their knowledge of curricular topics of study? Do they

- pose good questions for investigation?
- make reasonable hypotheses based on background knowledge and experience?
- make accurate and reliable observations?
- design their own investigations?
- collect and record data in tables, charts, diagrams, and graphs?
- use lab equipment effectively and efficiently?

- take accurate measurements?
- defend positions or viewpoints based on informed understandings?
- debate issues, weighing risks and benefits of different choices?
- apply new and existing knowledge to novel situations?
- keep meaningful records of their observations, procedures, drawings, hypotheses, data, interpretations, and questions?
- confidently make informed decisions based on scientific thought and experiment?

You will probably decide that performance tasks are the best assessment tools for skill and attitude outcomes. Traditional and common testing methods may not be sufficient to assess a student's ability to think about and choose methods for carrying out scientific inquiry. These assessment techniques may still prove useful, but each strategy must be carefully chosen to meet the intended purpose and goal.

Performance tasks may include designing and conducting an investigation, troubleshooting for a system that does not work, producing a written report or position paper, making a presentation, building a model, or creating a graphic representation. Each of these tasks requires students to consider what they know as well as the possible strategies for solving the problem. Rather than identifying the "correct answer," students must decide on the best approach, follow through, and reflect on the final process and product. *How* a student arrived at a solution is as important as the solution itself. The assessment, like the learning, is dynamic. It involves students in the metacognitive process.

The use of rubrics to evaluate performance tasks in science has gained new momentum. Unlike the past, where the odd "scoring guide" might have appeared within teacher support material (usually for lab reports or essays), today's textbook publishers produce rubrics for every possible activity! One rubric that was developed by science teachers and adapted to suit mathematics as well appears on pages 56 and 57.

As stated in other chapters, to make the use of rubrics metacognitive for students, actively involve them in modifying, adapting, and refining the rubrics. Ownership of the assessment process is critical if students are to progress along the continuum and work towards their goals. Experience has shown that rubrics are rarely final form. They evolve over time and with use. The inclusion of student exemplars (with permission and names removed) to illustrate different levels of performance helps students in assessing their own work and determining where they might improve. In becoming familiar with the scoring rubric and exemplars of performance, students consciously decide on the level of work they submit for peer review and final evaluation.

Enabling Students to Construct New Knowledge

In this chapter we examined two facets of metacognition in science: conceptual understanding (*how do I know what I know?*) and skill development (*how will I find out what I want to know?*).

How we learn is an important component of the philosophical movement in science education defined as "constructivism." The constructivist theory recognizes that teachers do not simply pour knowledge into empty student vessels. Learners construct knowledge based on previous understanding and experience. Children experience and test their surroundings from birth. They develop their own ideas and understandings of how and why the world works as it does. Some of these conceptions may be close to accepted scientific understanding; however, much of science is counter-intuitive, and students must be challenged to consider their own understandings in light of new evidence. If the evidence (from observation, investigation, and discussion) is compelling enough, new understandings will be constructed.

A learner who is accustomed to questioning and reflecting has a head start on constructing new knowledge supported by accumulated evidence. In *In Search of Understanding*, Jacqueline and Martin Brooks (1993) aptly state:

> A new set of images, reflective of new practices, is needed—images that portray the student as a thinker, a creator, and a constructor. Schools can become settings in which students are encouraged to develop hypotheses, to test out their own and other's ideas, to make connections among "content" areas, to explore issues and problems of personal relevance (either existing or emerging), to work cooperatively with peers and adults in the pursuit of understanding, and to form the disposition to be life-long learners. (1993, 126–27)

Students who act and learn in these ways are metacognitive.

5 Social Studies: A Way to Foster Informed Decision Making

A metacognitive focus to social studies methodology will add an important dimension to social studies instruction. Given that the ultimate goal of schools in general and social studies in particular is to develop responsible citizens, metacognition, which promotes learning how to learn, can play a valuable role in fostering lifelong learning. In 1916, the founding National Education Association's Committee on Social Studies stated that the "constant purpose" of social studies is the "cultivation of good citizenship" (Dougan 1988–89, 15). The development of effective programs to meet this goal has challenged social studies educators ever since.

Fostering Responsible Citizens

One of the most important traits of a good citizen in a democracy is the ability to make informed decisions. Citizens who have learned how to learn will be in a better position to use their knowledge and skills to find and process information in order to make decisions. In an article titled "Decision Making: The Heart of Social Studies," Shirley H. Engle stated, "in teaching the social studies, we should emphasize decision-making as against mere remembering." He further acknowledged that students are unlikely to become better decision makers unless "they receive guided and critically orientated exercises in the decision-making process" (1964, 28 and 32). By the 1970s, many social studies reformers settled on various inquiry models as the best systematic approach to achieve these goals.

Social studies inquiry can be defined as an approach to instruction that engages students in the search for solutions to problems in society. Joseph Kirman, in *Elementary Social Studies*, describes inquiry as a form of "structured reflective thinking" and as "a way of teaching where the child is involved in finding, evaluating, and applying information to a topic that is usually phrased as a problem or question" (1996, 19). Some inquiry models were designed for reflective inquiry with the focus on personal issues and values; others focused on social inquiry, exploring social policy issues, such as race relations or environmental problems. These models of inquiry were developed to provide structure for an idea that essentially defies structure. How does one capture the spirit of free and open inquiry with models that automatically seem to limit choice?

An ideal inquiry unit would be based on student interest. A student interested in a topic or issue will want to learn more and will explore ways of getting information to make a decision. Motivated students easily use a variety of learning strategies, many of which are highly metacognitive. However, when an inquiry process is locked in to pre-set inquiry issues, the process becomes a formula. It is the spirit, not the form, of inquiry that is important.

Perhaps a greater focus on metacognition would have prevented some of the basic problems that emerged as the inquiry approach went from theory to practice. The province of Alberta is a case in point. Alberta was the first Canadian province to jump on the inquiry process bandwagon. In 1971 the province introduced an inquiry-based social studies curriculum that proved highly controversial and ineffective. Students were invited to "free and open inquiry into the definition and application of social values" (page 5). Instead of teaching a Canadian History topic, for example, teachers were to help students examine a historical issue, such as national unity. The focus of instruction was on helping students gather information on the issue rather than teaching a history topic for the sake of learning about it.

The immediate concern by teachers was how to conduct open inquiry in the confines of a classroom and of the requirements of a mandatory curriculum. What if some students decided they did not want to inquire into the issue of national unity? Another serious charge against the curriculum was the question of teaching value relativism in public schools. For example, was it acceptable for a student to decide that national unity in Canada was a bad idea? By 1981, largely in reaction to the lack of structure in the program, social studies educators created a social inquiry process for the Alberta Social Studies Program of Studies. All students from Grades 1 to 12 were to follow these steps:

1. Identify and focus on the issue.
2. Establish research questions and procedures.
3. Gather and organize data.
4. Analyze and evaluate data.
5. Synthesize data.
6. Resolve the issue.
7. Apply the decision (or, postpone taking action).
8. Evaluate the decision and process.

While the document noted that the process was to be considered flexible, it was clearly intended to offer a "systematic approach to problem-solving while allowing for deviation in procedures" (page 7).

For many educators, the eight-step model quickly became dogma with little deviation. Inquiry was equated with getting the steps right. Thus, within ten years, the social studies program in Alberta went from unstructured, free, and open inquiry to a highly structured process of social inquiry. Both programs were flawed, but lessons about inquiry and metacognition can be learned from an analysis of these mistakes.

Reflecting on Past Inquiry Models

Ian Wright noted in *Elementary Social Studies* that if inquiry is viewed as rigid, "it can be just as deadening, mechanical, and passive as the worst form of exposition" (1991, 70). We need to *add* metacognition to our current understanding of the inquiry process, not replace the process. The goals of inquiry remain sound, but it is the practical application of the idea that makes all the difference. The 1981 Alberta example, for one, could have been greatly improved by a more deliberate focus on the principles of metacognitive instruction.

It is a question of approach and balance. If the focus of instruction is to ensure that the students learn the steps of inquiry, then that will likely happen. If, on the other hand, the focus is on the spirit of inquiry, students could easily miss some of the steps and content of a mandatory curriculum. *Genuine* inquiry, with deliberate metacognitive instruction, offers the best of both worlds. In such a classroom, students have a choice in identifying issues (step 1) and are encouraged to create their own research procedures (step 2). They then have a large say in conducting the research (steps 3, 4, and 5). Having had a say in what and how they learned (steps 6 and 7), they would then be in a better position to evaluate their learning (step 8). This kind of application of the inquiry process in social studies would be a good start in helping students learn how to learn.

Allowing Issues for Inquiry to Emerge

Developing a metacognitive inquiry unit requires adaptation of some aspects of the inquiry process. The study of issues is central to any inquiry-based social studies program; however, using generalized pre-packaged issues as unit organizers is a mistake. Social studies units and plans should be based on content topics, not on general issues. An issue, by definition, is something about which people disagree and wish to argue. If no one cares, there is no issue! Students and teachers need a choice in the matter; otherwise, the inquiry becomes a meaningless exercise.

Issues and problems for inquiry will emerge naturally from the study of required content. Instead of using an organizing issue such as "How should the explorers, missionaries, fur traders, and settlers in Canada's early history have interacted with each other?" the topic of study should be Early Settlers. As students learn about the topic, the issue of interaction probably would emerge. At that point, when interest is high, the students could conduct an inquiry into the issue. Inquiry instruction is best viewed as a process, not as a set of steps, with issues a natural development from topics of study. This understanding is a first step to metacognitive inquiry.

A sample unit with a metacognitive dimension

Issues that emerge from the study of content can form the basis for student inquiry. For example, if the curriculum topic is Early Settlement in Canada, the teacher might plan and present a lesson on the Loyalists, the largest group of settlers in Upper Canada (Ontario) after the American Revolution. While learning about the Loyalists, some students may ask why they were called Loyalists. As discussion on this question gets under way, some of them may wonder if the Loyalists were considered traitors to the American Revolution. Others may argue that these settlers were Loyalists because they remained loyal to the king of England—free land in the British colonies in the north was their reward. As the interest and debate on the question heat up, the teacher could suggest that the students prepare a formal debate: "Be it resolved that the United Empire Loyalists receive free land in recognition of their loyalty to the Crown during the American Revolution." An alternative to the debating format is to develop an issue statement for the class. For example: "Should the Loyalists be considered heroes or traitors?" Each student would then be directed to develop a position on the issue and write a position paper. Thus, a single history lesson can lead to a much larger inquiry unit.

To ensure a metacognitive dimension to this activity, the teacher should ask the students to identify and consider various research and presentation strategies for developing a position. Research options could include the use of library reference books, CD-ROMs, textbooks, Internet sources tied to historical societies, and interviews with local historians. These research options may not be readily apparent to students so it is important for teachers to build a repertoire of research strategies for students. The students should also have a choice of presentation formats, such as an essay, a collage, a poster set in the historical time period, a cartoon, a PowerPoint presentation, or participation in a formal debate.

At key points in the inquiry process and at the conclusion of this activity, students would be given time to reflect on what and how they are studying the topic. This time for conscious reflection is the key to metacognitive inquiry.

Students could be asked to sum up their reflections in their notebooks for future reference.

Endless issues surface from the study of required social studies content. History topics, in particular, are rich in controversy: for example, the study of Aboriginal Treaties, the Vietnam War, and the War on Terrorism. Issues in geography are also easy to find. A study of regional Canadian geography, for example, is likely to raise this question: "Should the rich regions of Canada be required to share their wealth?" Teachers must teach the required curriculum topics, but selecting specific issues and determining how to proceed with their study can be student based.

Adding opportunities for choice at key points will help achieve the goals of metacognitive inquiry, but is only the start. Most students do not know how to identify issues, create research procedures, and so on. They need help and direction from teachers. Margaret C. Wang and Anne Marie Palincsar, cited in an article for the National Council for the Social Studies, noted that to achieve metacognitive goals, students need to learn "strategies, or rules for successful problem solving and completion of new tasks, and an understanding of how one's own learning characteristics interact with the learning environment" (1991, 125). The trick is to show students how to do it without locking the process into a meaningless set of steps where the means become confused with the ends.

Writing a Position Paper

Perhaps the most powerful tool for social studies instruction is writing a position paper. The position paper is a comprehensive and concrete expression of a student's ability to apply knowledge and skills, such as gathering and organizing information, evaluating information, identifying and evaluating the quality of arguments and supporting evidence, separating facts from opinions, developing a position on an issue and defending it persuasively.

The writing of a position paper is essentially a presentation of an argument. Richard Fulkerson, in *Teaching the Argument in Writing,* upholds the importance of argument in a free society (1996, ix). He further notes that the point of argumentation is to reach "wise decisions"—surely the goal of responsible citizens.

The position paper in social studies may be quite different than persuasive writing papers in other subjects. The key difference is in the nature and use of evidence to support the position. Evidence and persuasiveness come in many forms and have a different currency in different subjects. Most marks for a position paper are given for the defence of the position, not for the mechanics of writing. Evidence can include hard facts, such as names, dates, and statistics, but the key to a good social studies paper is often in the effective use of "soft" information, such as opinions of authorities in the field and the use of logical arguments. Quoting an authority or a statement from a reputable newspaper can do much to strengthen a position paper. Social studies papers draw on a wide range of information.

Writing a position paper has a metacognitive dimension in that students can approach the writing in a variety of ways. Students who learn best visually should try finding films and television documentaries on the topic of study. Some will write several drafts of each section, while others will prefer to build a final draft as a whole. Many writers start in the middle with the basic information, then build outwards to the opening and closing paragraphs. Most writers will begin with the strongest argument first, then include weaker arguments; in some cases, however, the opposite way can work just as well. The point is: *the product is given, but the process to get there can be varied*.

Marking such a paper is difficult unless the writing expectations are set clearly. Students who move from class to class soon realize that a paper is not a paper—it depends on the subject and sometimes on the teacher. Teachers should understand that writing assignments are tied to specific requirements and that they have a responsibility to teach students the specific skills required to complete the task.

Using scoring guides in assessment

Teachers using metacognitive inquiry strategies, such as the writing of a position paper, will need to consider appropriate assessments. For the writing of a position paper, teachers would probably find the use of self-evaluation scoring guides valuable. To add a metacognitive dimension, ask students to adapt the scoring guide for themselves and have you approve it. Or, ask the class to work together to create a scoring guide for a term paper. A sample scoring guide is provided on the next page. Students would complete it and include it with their paper.

An alternative to the scoring guide is the Argumentative Essay Checklist which appears on page 80. Criteria that are outlined on the Argumentative Essay Checklist should be discussed with students to ensure that they understand what each of the statements mean. Students should also be invited to suggest changes to the list.

Rubrics are a powerful assessment tool. Examples of rubrics for writing can be found wherever standardized tests require a writing sample. Many textbooks also include these in their assessment strategies. Sample rubrics can be used as guides for the construction of rubrics for classroom assignments. Ideally, students should be asked to participate in the development of rubrics for writing assignments.

Student Scoring Guide

Content   **Value**

_____ Does my introduction present the topic or issue in an interesting way?   ___ / 35

_____ Are my arguments clearly stated?

_____ Do my supporting examples and evidence support my argument?

_____ Have I used appropriate vocabulary from social studies content?

_____ Is my conclusion clear?

_____ Have I clearly restated my position in the conclusion?

Organization

_____ Is the issue clearly stated in the introduction?   ___ / 10

_____ Is my position clearly stated in the introduction?

_____ Do I provide strong supporting information and examples?

_____ Does my conclusion include my position on the issue?

Mechanics of Writing

_____ Have I used persuasive language, such as adjectives and verbs?   ___ / 5

_____ Have I used a variety of sentences?

_____ Have I used correct grammar, capitalization, and punctuation?

_____ Are my words spelled correctly?

Total: ___ / 50

Argumentative Essay Checklist

❑ 1.   I have clearly explained the background to the issue.

❑ 2.   My argument is clearly stated.

❑ 3.   I use appropriate evidence and reasons to support my argument.

❑ 4.   I recognize and refute the key counter arguments.

❑ 5.   My paper has a logical flow to it.

❑ 6.   I use at least one quote in my paper.

❑ 7.   I have used effective language and expressions.

❑ 8.   I have concluded with a strong statement.

❑ 9.   I have checked for spelling and grammar.

❑ 10. I have cited all sources used in the paper.

Teaching History Through the Interpretive Approach

History is more than a record of the past; it is an interpretation of the past record. When interpretations differ, controversy arises. Controversial issues are fueled by research as new evidence emerges and insights are discovered. Authorities line up on different sides of an issue and write articles and books reflecting their views. The Interpretive Approach (IA) is designed to help teachers and students use argumentative articles and books to learn more about the issue in question and to provide students with good models for writing a position paper. By analyzing and evaluating such writing, students get practice in the skills of persuasive writing. They will see examples of experts stating and defending a position with effective use of evidence.

These are the key steps in the IA strategy:

1. Understand the background information to the event.
2. Understand the key interpretations of the event.
3. Analyze and evaluate different interpretations of the event.
4. Develop a personal position on the interpretations of the event.

The Cold War: An example of the IA strategy

1. Understand the background information to the event.
Let us assume the topic of study is the Cold War. In the course of studying the Cold War, students read several sources covering Churchill's "Iron Curtain" speech in 1946, the Truman Doctrine (1947), the Berlin Blockade, the formation of the North Atlantic Treaty Organization (NATO), and other events leading to the hardening of positions between the two new superpowers, the United States and the Soviet Union. For the fifty years following World War II, the world was divided by the threat of nuclear war. Why did that happen? Who was responsible for the breakdown in the relationship between the United States and the Soviet Union? The teacher asks the students to consider the question "Was the United States or the Soviet Union responsible for the outbreak of the Cold War?"

2. Understand the key interpretations of the event.
This question is complex so it is easier to turn to the experts for their insights. The main problem for teachers is to find clear, concise readings on both sides of the question. For this question, the teacher could use an excerpt from *The Long Peace,* by John Lewis Geddis, for one viewpoint and *Meeting the Communist Threat: Truman to Reagan*, by Thomas G. Paterson, for an opposing view.* Geddis argues

---

* Examples of these articles, adapted for students, are available in *Twentieth Century Viewpoints: An Interpretive History* by V. Zelinski, G. Draper, D. Quinlan, and F. McFadden (Toronto: Oxford University Press).

that unilateral actions by the Soviets caused the Cold War. Paterson argues that the United States was to blame because the Americans exaggerated Soviet actions and launched a policy of containment which isolated and angered the Soviets.

3. Analyze and evaluate the different interpretations of the event.
At this point, each student completes an argument analysis and evaluation of each article.

The form that appears on page 83 will help the students to complete the task.

4. Develop a personal position on the interpretations of the event.
After completing the analysis of both readings, the students will decide which of the different positions they accept and why. They then prepare a short position paper on the question using their prior knowledge of the Cold War and the arguments by the two authors.

Conducting an Article Review

An alternative strategy for the critical examination of argumentative articles is to conduct an article review. This strategy requires students to read an article and determine the main viewpoint and the key reasons and evidence supporting the argument. The students conclude with a paragraph stating their opinion of the article.

From a metacognitive point of view, students need both direction and choice. The IA and article review strategies should be taught as examples of different ways to analyze and evaluate argumentative articles. Teachers should collect other strategies to achieve the same goal and teach as many of these as possible to the students. (The Recommended Resources section near the end of this book features several good sources describing a wide range of strategies for elementary and secondary teachers.) As the students gain competence in the use of these strategies, they will be better able to choose strategies for learning that best meet their needs.

Adding a Metacognitive Dimension to Projects

Metacognition can be readily added to regular social studies projects and activities.

Tarry Lindquist and Douglas Selwyn offer an interesting example of a structured activity with a built-in metacognitive dimension. The Model House Project, which appears in *Social Studies at the Center*, can be part of a unit on settlers and immigration. Students are asked to construct an accurate model of a house in which an immigrant to North America may have lived before emigrating. In part I of this project, Lindquist and Selwyn provide focus questions for gathering information

Argument Analysis and Evaluation Summary

Author and Reading _____

_____

Question/Issue_____

1. Identify the main argument (viewpoint) in the article.

    _____

    _____

2. Identify the evidence used to support the argument.

    _____

    _____

    _____

    _____

    _____

    _____

3. Evaluate the argument. Do you tend to agree or disagree with the author?

    _____

    _____

    _____

    _____

    _____

    _____

4. Develop a personal position on this interpretation of the event.

    _____

    _____

    _____

    _____

    _____

and research. For example: Where is your character from? What is the weather like? What materials would be used for the house? Describe the land. The questions in part II, however, are quite different. In this part, called "Reflections on the Model Project," students respond to questions like these: What did I enjoy most about the project? What did I do that was most helpful? What would I do different next time? What did I learn about this project? These are metacognitive questions that promote personal reflection about learning. Here, students think about themselves as learners as opposed to what they learned (see pages 253–56 of the book for the full example).

Making Inquiry Dynamic

Inquiry-based instruction has taken strong root in social studies education; however, recognizing the need to deliberately add a metacognitive dimension to inquiry is still an emerging trend. The main argument in this chapter is that metacognition is an essential ingredient for inquiry instruction. Without it, good inquiry models, strategies, and practices, such as the Interpretive Approach, can easily lose the spirit of inquiry and become fossilized as formulae. Metacognition makes inquiry work.

Metacognition, like inquiry, must be taught in context, not as a discrete list of skills. Since learning is always about something, learning how to learn in any school subject requires students to be familiar with the essential ways of learning in the subject. Inquiry can be viewed as the best route for social studies instruction, but, by itself, is not always enough. This chapter has described some of the pitfalls of locking inquiry into a set of steps or a formula.

Metacognitive inquiry, on the other hand, adds metacognition to the inquiry process. Its strategies engage students in structured learning activities that lead to effective learning outcomes along with thoughtful reflection. Structure is necessary for effective learning, but structure should also be flexible and reflective. This chapter has outlined several practical strategies and classroom activities that attempt to combine both structure and flexibility. They are intended to serve as practical and effective examples of metacognitive inquiry.

A Final Word:
A Model for Professional Development

As advocates of the value of metacognition, we have worked with teachers interested in coordinating their focus on metacognition across grades and subjects. Our experience with these projects suggests a professional development model that may be useful for other groups.

Once teachers express an interest in learning more about thinking and metacognition, in particular, they might begin a shared exploration of the topic. One way is to engage an "expert" speaker, especially one able to discuss metacognition in terms of a specific subject area. An alternative is a reading group approach to this resource, *I Think, Therefore I Learn!* After reading part of the book, colleagues could note positive and negative aspects of a focus on metacognition. They could follow this exercise by discussing ways to promote metacognition in their students and encourage helpful parental support.

Collecting appropriate assessment data is a critical component of any professional development effort among teaching colleagues. When teachers see evidence that students learn better due to thoughtful reflection on what they do before, during, and after working on a task, they will strengthen their commitment to the professional development focus.

However, before that happens, it is worthwhile to create a "We agree" statement to consolidate the group's professional development focus. Some schools have published such a statement in newsletters; others have framed and displayed the statement in the school. Here is one representative example:

> In our school, we will work together to help students identify their thinking about thinking before, during, and after important tasks and projects. We will encourage students to identify specific strategies that they will use to complete tasks.

Such a statement reminds a school community about its current professional development target. Without a doubt, metacognition is a worthwhile focus.

SMALL-GROUP WORK STUDENT ASSESSMENT FORM

Criteria   *My Goals for Small-Group Work*

_____ 1. I helped the group review its task.

_____ 2. I contributed relevant ideas; I stayed on
           topic.

_____ 3. I listened carefully to other group
           members.

_____ 4. I was open-minded about different
           interpretations or understandings.

_____ 5. I helped the group stay focused on its task.

_____ 6. I contributed to the summary which
           concluded the group work.

_____ 7. I encouraged all members of the group
           to contribute.

A Parental Guide to Promoting Reflective Learning

A common question that parents pose to teachers is "When it comes to schoolwork, how can I help and encourage my child?" There are many subject-specific suggestions to assist parents; here, however, let us focus on learning in a broader sense.

Begin by considering the strengths that *you* bring to tackling a new task or problem.

- What would you identify as your greatest skills? For example, if you do crosswords, you may have an extensive vocabulary; perhaps you have a talent for painting watercolours; perhaps you are good at planning and organizing events; or maybe you work effectively in groups.

- Do you spend time analyzing the situation, or are you most effective when you jump right in?

- Can you identify a variety of strategies that you use in different situations? For example, perhaps you regularly use lists for planning, use graphic organizers and sketches to represent ideas, make pictures in your mind while reading, or tell a group your understanding of what members have agreed on. When has each strategy been most useful to you?

- Have others commented or noticed certain strategies, methods, or approaches that you employ that they find admirable, effective, or unusual?

- Have you noticed strategies used by others that you would like to learn or employ? Do your children demonstrate strategies (perhaps learned in school) that you are unfamiliar with and would like to learn?

As a parent, you have much to offer your child by building on your strengths and recognizing that there are other approaches yet to learn and master. The constant teacher in your child's life, you have the ability to guide your child as a reflective learner above and beyond the school curriculum.

Resist the temptation to provide *the* answer or *the* steps/method/approach whenever your child asks. You may find that very difficult to do. Parents' first response is often to pass on "knowledge" in an attempt to make things easier or less complicated for their children, but you should instead bite your tongue.

You are at a critical and exciting juncture. Seize the moment! Be open and creative with your child, and enjoy learning *from* your child. Ask questions and listen. Then model *your* strengths and strategies by talking about them out loud. The following chart may help you to get started.

Ask Your Child	Ask Yourself	Share with Your Child
• What do you think this problem/task is all about? • How did you determine that?	• Is my child's perspective the same as mine? Have I seen the problem/task in a different way?	• State to your child your understanding of the problem/task and explain how you came to that determination.
• How do you think you will approach this task? • Can you explain why you chose that method? • What do you already know, or what are you good at, that will help you to complete this task? • Is there anything new that you need to know or be able to do to help you to complete this task?	• How would I approach the task? Can I explain why? When do the rules/methods I have chosen work, and when not? • What do I already know, or what am I good at, that affects the choices I would make? • Is there any other strategy possible that neither of us has thought of yet?	• Share your ideas about what you already know and are good at that would affect the choices you would make. • If your child has chosen a different strategy from yours, invite your child to teach it to you.
• How will you explain or show your work to everyone else? • Why did you choose that method? • How do you know it is appropriate for the task? • Would you have done it this way even if the teacher hadn't "said so"? Why?	• Can I think of an equally good method of communicating the work?	• Consider that your child's work may be communicated in a variety of forms depending on the nature of the task (e.g., through oral language, written language, graphs, diagrams, and charts). • If you can think of an equally good method of communicating the work, discuss it with your child.

Explore with your child the *how* and *why* of choices made in solving problems or meeting new challenges. In doing so, your child will become better able to assess a new task and determine the strengths and strategies necessary to complete it. And so will you. Being able to think this way will bring success in school—and in life.

References by Chapter

1 A Powerful Way of Thinking

Bloom, B. S. 1956. *Taxonomy of Educational Objectives.* New York: Longmans Green.

Bransford, John D., Ann L. Brown, and Rodney R. Cocking, eds. 2000. *How People Learn.* Washington, D.C.: National Academy Press.

Conference Board of Canada. Employability Skills 2000+.

Foster, Graham. 1996. *Student Self-Assessment: A Powerful Process for Helping Students Revise Their Writing.* Markham, ON: Pembroke Publishers.

Gardner, Howard. 1993. *Multiple Intelligences: The Theory and the Practice.* New York: HarperCollins.

Scruggs, Thomas, M. A. Mastopier, J. Monson, and C. Jorgenson. "Maximizing What Gifted Students Can Learn: Recent Findings of Learning Strategy Research." *Gifted Child Quarterly* (Fall 1985): 181–85.

2 Language Arts: A Way to Know Self and World

Alberta Education. 1996. *Programming for Students with Special Needs.* Book 6. Edmonton, AB.

Ellefson, Bryan, Graham Foster, Ann Manson, and Janeen Werner-King. 2000. *Performance Assessment: Encouraging Student Success and Establishing Standards.* English Language Arts Program of Studies K–9 Orientation: Session 4. Series prepared for Alberta Regional Consortium.

Hillocks, George, Jr. 1986. *Research on Written Composition, New Directions in Teaching.* Urbana, IL: National Council of Teachers of English.

Hinson, Bess, ed. 2000. *New Directions in Reading Instruction.* Rev. ed. Newark, DE: International Reading Association.

Rosenblatt, Louise. 1956. "The Acid Test for Literature Instruction." *English Journal* 45: 66–74.

3   Mathematics: A Way to Deepen Understanding

Alberta Education. June 1996. Alberta Program of Studies for K–9 Mathematics. Western Canadian Protocol.

Ginsburg, Herbert P., Susan F. Jacobs, and Luz S. Lopez. 1993. "Assessing Mathematical Thinking and Learning Potential." In *Schools, Mathematics, and the World of Reality,* edited by Robert B. Davis and Carolyn S. Maher, pp. 237–62. Boston: Allyn and Bacon.

Hiebert, J. C., T. P. Carpenter, E. Fennema, K. C. Fuson, D. Wearne, H. G. Murray, A. I. Olivier, and P. G. Human. 1997. *Making Sense: Teaching and Learning Mathematics with Understanding.* Portsmouth, N.H.: Heinemann.

Higgins, J. 1988. "We Get What We Ask For." *Arithmetic Teacher* 5: 2.

National Council of Supervisors of Mathematics. 1997. *Supporting Improvement in Mathematics Education.* Golden, CO: NCSM.

National Council of Teachers of Mathematics. 2000. *Principles and Standards for School Mathematics.* Reston, VA: NCTM.

National Council of Teachers of Mathematics. 1991. *Professional Standards for Teaching Mathematics.* Reston, VA: NCTM.

National Council of Teachers of Mathematics. 1980. *An Agenda for Action: Recommendations for School Mathematics of the 1980s.* Reston, VA: NCTM.

Polya, George. 1957. *How to Solve It.* Princeton, N.J.: Princeton University Press.

4   Science: A Way to Reconstruct Knowledge

Annenberg/CPB Math and Science Collection Video. 1997. "Minds of Our Own: Lessons from Thin Air." Burlington, VT: President and Fellows of Harvard College.

Brooks, Jacqueline Grennon, and Martin G. Brooks. 1993. *In Search of Understanding: The Case for Constructivist Classrooms.* Alexandria, VA: Association for Supervision and Curriculum Development.

Council of Ministers of Education, Canada. 1997. *Common Framework of Science Learning Outcomes: Pan-Canadian Protocol for Collaboration on School Curriculum.* Toronto: Council of Ministers of Education, Canada.

Dart, B. C., et al. 1998. "Change in Knowledge of Learning and Teaching Through Journal Writing." *Research Papers in Education* 13(3): 291–318.

DeBoer, George E. 2000. "Scientific Literacy: Another Look at Its Historical and Contemporary Meanings and Its Relationship to Science Education Reform." *Journal of Research in Science Teaching* 37(6): 582–601.

McKay, John P., Bennett D. Hill, and John Buckler. 1995. *A History of Western Society.* Toronto: Houghton Mifflin.

National Research Council. 1996. *National Science Education Standards.* Washington, D.C.: National Academy Press.

Science Council of Canada. 1984. *Report 36: Science for Every Student. Educating Canadians for Tomorrow's World.* Hull: Canadian Government Publishing Centre.

Wiggins, Grant, and Jay McTighe. 1998. *Understanding by Design.* Alexandria, VA: Association for Supervision and Curriculum Development.

5 Social Studies: A Way to Foster Informed Decision Making

Alberta Social Studies Program of Studies. 1981. Edmonton, AB: Alberta Education.

Alberta Social Studies Program of Studies. 1971. Edmonton, AB: Department of Education.

Alleman, Janet Elaine, and Cheryl L. Rosen. 1991. "The Cognitive, Social-Emotional, and Moral Development Characteristics of Students: Basis for Elementary and Middle School Social Studies." In *Handbook of Research on Social Studies Teaching and Learning*, edited by James P. Shaver. National Council for the Social Studies. New York: Macmillan.

Dougan, Alberta M. 1988/89. "Social Studies: Old Masters and Founders." *International Journal of Social Education* 3 (winter): 15.

Engle, Shirley H. 1964. "Decision Making: The Heart of Social Studies." In *Crucial Studies in the Teaching of Social Studies: A Book of Readings,* edited by B. Massialas and A. Kazamias. Englewood Cliffs, N.J.: Prentice-Hall.

Fulkerson, Richard. 1996. *Teaching the Argument in Writing.* Urbana, IL: National Council of Teachers of English.

Kirman, Joseph. 1996. *Elementary Social Studies.* 2d ed. Scarborough, ON: Allyn and Bacon Canada.

Lindquist, Tarry, and Douglas Selwyn. 2000. *Social Studies at the Center: Integrating Kids, Content, and Literacy.* Portsmouth, N.H.: Heinemann.

Wright, Ian D. 1991. *Elementary Social Studies: A Practical Approach to Teaching and Learning.* 3rd ed. Scarborough, ON: Nelson Canada.

Recommended Resources

Bransford, John D., Ann L. Brown, and Rodney R. Cocking. 2000. *How People Learn*. Washington, D.C.: National Academy Press.

How People Learn usefully explores the thinking processes of experts and non-experts, or novices, as they complete learning tasks. The examples from mathematics and science are particularly helpful to illustrate the value of metacognitive activities incorporated into subject matter instruction.

Case, Roland, and Penny Clark. 1997. *The Canadian Anthology of Social Studies: Issues and Strategies for the Teacher*. Burnaby, B.C.: Simon Fraser University Press.

This collection of articles written by Canadian social studies educators emphasizes student ownership of social studies learning.

Cook, Doris. 1989. *Strategic Learning in the Content Areas*. Madison, WS: Wisconsin Department of Public Education.

This practical resource reviews a range of learning strategies with an emphasis on independent monitoring by students. It is particularly strong in its attention to reading and writing strategies.

Costa, Art. 2000. *Habits of Mind: A Developmental Series*. Alexandria, VA: Association for Supervision and Curriculum Development.

This series stresses the value of understanding oneself as a learner and discusses what teachers can do to engage and sustain metacognition.

Dweck. C. S. 1999. *Self-Theories: Their Role in Motivation, Personality, and Development*. Philadelphia, PA: Psychology Press.

This accessible text discusses how beliefs that students have about themselves affect their learning.

Foster, Graham. 1996. *Student Self-Assessment: A Powerful Process for Helping Students Revise Their Writing.* Markham, ON: Pembroke Publishers.

The book promotes metacognition through independent student self-assessment and related goal setting in writing.

Grant, Janet Millar, Barbara Heffler, and Kadri Mereweather. 1995. *Student-Led Conferences: Using Portfolios to Share Learning with Parents.* Markham, ON: Pembroke Publishers.

The book emphasizes how portfolios and student-led conferences help students take responsibility for their own learning—a major characteristic of metacognition.

Hemmerich, Hal, Wendy Lim, and Kanwal Neel. 1994. *Prime Time: Strategies for Lifelong Learning in Mathematics and Science in the Middle and High School Grades.* Markham, ON: Pembroke Publishers.

This practical resource emphasizes active learning with student attention to strategies required to complete a task.

Hinson, Bess, ed. 2000. *New Directions in Reading Instruction.* Rev. ed. Newark, DE: International Reading Association.

In this practical book, metacognition through student awareness and control of their reading strategies is stressed.

Kirman, Joseph M. 1986. *Elementary Social Studies.* 2d ed. Scarborough, ON: Allyn and Bacon.

Chapter 3 usefully discusses learning, thinking, and metacognition in social studies.

Kovach, Karen. 1999. *A Collection of the Best Learning Strategies on Earth.* 2d ed. Edmonton, AB: Academic Support Centre, University of Alberta Press.

Written for students, this book challenges students to employ specific strategies characteristic of successful learners.

Lake, Jo-Anne. 1997. *Lifelong Learning Skills: How to Teach Today's Children for Tomorrow's Challenges.* Markham, ON: Pembroke Publishers.

The book's focus on lifelong learning attends to both skills and strategies valued by employers. Its emphasis on students taking responsibility for their learning is metacognitive.

Lindquist, Tarry, and Douglas Selwyn. 2000. *Social Studies at the Center: Integrating Kids, Content, and Literacy.* Portsmouth, NH: Heinemann.

Chapter 5 outlines 68 practical teaching strategies that engage students in meaningful, student-centred social studies activities.

Parsons, Les. 2001. *Response Journals Revisited.* Markham, ON: Pembroke Publishers.

The book's central topic of self-understanding and connecting personal experiences to text underlines the metacognitive value of response journals.

Wright, Ian. 1991. *Elementary Social Studies: A Practical Approach to Teaching and Learning.* Scarborough, ON: Nelson Canada.

Wright's focus on practical teaching suggestions based on critical thinking about one's social studies teaching emphasizes independent thinking by students.

Index